"A book like this is not written b̶̶̶̶̶̶̶̶̶̶̶̶̶̶̶̶ ̶̶̶̶̶̶̶̶̶̶̶̶̶̶̶ ̶̶̶̶̶̶̶̶̶̶̶̶̶̶̶̶ ̶̶̶̶̶̶̶̶̶̶ ̶̶̶̶ ̶̶̶̶̶̶ and quality materials. Jenny walks with hurting wives into the fire and through the long wait, following the precious truth of God's compassion and power. Her guidance is careful, honest, and confident in the Lord. Simply excellent."

Jeremy Pierre, Lawrence and Charlotte Hoover Professor of Biblical Counseling & Department Chair, The Southern Baptist Theological Seminary; author of *The Dynamic Heart in Daily Life* and *When Home Hurts*

"Curtis and Jenny Solomon's books, written as husband and wife to husbands and wives in the throes of pornography's sobering devastation, provide gentle yet sinewy and personal encouragement and guidance. Reading these books felt like sitting with trustworthy companions for couples who need Christ's courage and hope regarding repentance and freedom from porn and the pain it brings to marriages."

Ellen Mary Dykas, Director of Women's Ministry, Harvest USA; author of *Sexual Sanity for Women* and *Toxic Relationships*; coauthor of *Sexual Faithfulness*

"This is one of the most important books any married couple will read. Take in these truths and let them encourage you, strengthen you, and challenge you to fight for what matters most: each other."

Chad M. Robichaux, Founder, Mighty Oaks Foundation

"Jenny Solomon writes as someone who has been there and offers you her sorrow, compassion, and kindness. She also writes as one who has seen Christ do what seemed impossible and offers you her wisdom, clarity, and confidence. Pick it up and read it—you'll be glad you took advantage of her offer to help guide you through your and your spouse's painful and personal struggles."

Nathanael Brooks, Assistant Professor of Christian Counseling, Reformed Theological Seminary, Charlotte, NC

"If your husband struggles with pornography, look no further. Jenny Solomon is a wise, thoughtful, Christ-centered, and trustworthy guide. She's honest about her own struggles and she cares about wives who face the difficulties of an addicted husband. Does God offer strength, wisdom, and hope to a wife who suffers under the weight of her husband's addiction? Absolutely yes. This book will help you to see that much more clearly."

Deepak Reju, Pastor of Biblical Counseling and Family Ministry, Capitol Hill Baptist Church, Washington, DC; author of *Pornography: Fighting for Purity* and coauthor of *Rescue Plan: Charting a Course to Restore Prisoners of Pornography*

"Curtis and Jenny have much wisdom to share with couples who are hurting as a result of one partner's use of porn. I would encourage couples to learn from them how to glorify Jesus in the midst of great hurt."

Amy Baker, Ministry Resource Director at Faith Church, Lafayette, IN; author of *Getting to the Heart of Friendships* and *Picture Perfect*; editor of *Caring for the Souls of Children*

"Jenny Solomon's book, *Reclaim Your Marriage*, is an invitation to address sexual brokenness honestly and carefully with grace and truth. It is an ideal conversation starter for uncomfortable and hurtful areas."

Gregg R. Allison, Professor of Christian Theology, The Southern Baptist Theological Seminary; secretary, Evangelical Theological Society; author of *Embodied: Living as Whole People in a Fractured World*

"There are few books aimed directly at women who struggle with husbands who view pornography. Jenny Solomon adds a much-needed voice to this discussion. Readers will be drawn in through her vulnerability and will deepen their understanding of how Scripture speaks to this issue."

Jonathan D. Holmes, Executive Director, Fieldstone Counseling; coauthor of *Rescue Plan* and *Rescue Skills*

"Written with the tenderness and earned wisdom of one who knows this suffering, Jenny has given us an invaluable resource for hurting wives, one that seeks to strengthen their faith for the uncertain journey ahead."

Darby Strickland, Faculty member, The Christian Counseling and Educational Foundation (CCEF); author of *Is it Abuse?*

"I am certain that this new pair of books by my friends Curtis and Jenny Solomon will serve many couples as they redeem and reclaim a marriage that has been harmed by pornography. Those who read these books will find them helpful, challenging, encouraging, and best of all, biblical."

Tim Challies, Blogger at Challies.com; author of *Epic: An Around-the-World Journey through Christian History*

Reclaim
Your Marriage

Grace for Wives Who Have Been
Hurt by Pornography

Jenny Solomon

New
Growth
Press
newgrowthpress.com

New Growth Press, Greensboro, NC 27401
newgrowthpress.com

Cover Design: Faceout Books, faceoutstudios.com
Interior Typesetting: Lisa Parnell, lparnellbookservices.com

ISBN: 978-1-64507-227-0 (Print)

ISBN: 978-1-64507-228-7 (eBook)

Library of Congress Cataloging-in-Publication Data
Names: Solomon, Jenny, author.

Title: Reclaim your marriage : grace for wives who have been hurt by
pornography / by Jenny Solomon.

Description: Greensboro, NC : New Growth Press, [2022] | Includes
bibliographical references and index. | Summary: "Jenny Solomon comes
alongside hurting wives and gently encourages them to bring their pain to
God"— Provided by publisher.

Identifiers: LCCN 2021051744 (print) | LCCN 2021051745 (ebook) | ISBN
9781645072270 (print) | ISBN 9781645072287 (ebook)

Subjects: LCSH: Marriage—Religious aspects—Christianity. | Pornography—
Religious aspects—Christianity. | Wives—Religious life. | Husbands—Sexual
behavior.

Classification: LCC BV835 .S625 2022 (print) | LCC BV835 (ebook) |
DDC 248.8/44—dc23/eng/20211208

LC record available at https://lccn.loc.gov/2021051744

LC ebook record available at https://lccn.loc.gov/2021051745

Printed in the United States of America

29 28 27 26 25 24 23 22   1 2 3 4 5

TO MY FRIEND,

Andrea Lee:

YOUR ENTHUSIASTIC ATTENTION
LENT ME COURAGE TO HONE THE EARLY
DRAFTS. THIS BOOK IS WISER BECAUSE OF YOU.

Contents

Foreword

NO BRIDE WHO pledges her heart, body, and life on her wedding day is imagining a day when she'll pick up a book like this one. When she pledged to keep herself only for her beloved, she couldn't imagine herself trying to figure out a way to breathe again after the emotional blows delivered by the one who promised to love and cherish her. She trusted him with the most intimate details of her personhood. He's seen things and knows things about her that no one else has seen or known. And he has desecrated them. He has seen them and mingled them with the images, sounds, and desires of other women, virtual or not.

Was she not enough? Was her love, her body, her response, her faithfulness, worth so little to him? Could she have done better? Is this her fault? She remembers all the times he told her she was beautiful—that he loved her. And then she remembers what he has done. And she questions everything about him, about them, their past, and their future. How much of this was a lie?

Pain she never imagined is now indelibly etched on her heart. Will she ever forget? Will she ever forgive? Should she? Will she ever again trust that the words he once spoke to her are worth believing? And if he's lied about this, what else is he lying about?

The ground that once felt so solid, so secure, so *right*, has become quicksand under her feet.

If this is your story, what you've experienced is nothing less than a betrayal. Betrayal is also something that your pure and holy Savior felt. It came at the hand of his friend Judas. But Judas wasn't the only one. His dear companion Peter denied that he even knew him. The people from his hometown scoffed at his ministry. Those who were "his own" didn't receive him (John 1:11). He understands betrayal—*on every level*. Those who promised they would be stalwart, faithful, and courageous deserted him in his time of greatest need. He has felt what you're feeling. He doesn't just know because he's the omniscient God; he knows because he lived it.

Jesus wasn't like other men. He never once looked at a woman with lust in his heart. He never looked at her breasts and wanted to take them for his own pleasure. When women kissed his feet or anointed him with costly perfume, he never thought, *not even once*, "I'm going to get me some of that." He's the one man among all men who loved unselfishly, unreservedly. He never thought a woman should lose some weight or spend more time on herself to make herself attractive to him. Never once. And it's to you, to the women who are his that he now says, "Cast your burden on me. I will sustain you. You feel like you're drowning, but I've got you. And I understand."

Let me also say that, like Jenny Solomon, I understand the pain of a husband's use of porn. Jenny's story is mine as well. And we're not alone. Since 64 percent of Christian men admit to using porn, more than half of your sisters in church understand what you're walking through, too.

I'm thankful for this book on many levels. I'm thankful that Jenny has chosen this path of humility and transparency. I'm thankful that she loves the Lord and has fought to love her husband, Curtis, through all the disillusionment, pain, and betrayal that comes with porn use. I'm thankful that Curtis is humble enough to encourage her to write this book for you and that he allowed her to uncover his sin. Jenny's willingness to write this book is one of the most courageous acts of love I've seen lately. I'm also thankful that Jenny loves the Lord the way she does and that his Word has been a rock and a lamp to her. Her testimony is beautiful.

I've frequently wondered how the revolting scourge of pornography use by Christians can be stopped. I doubt that learning how damaging it is to one's soul will stop it—though that is true. I know that laws prohibiting it won't change anything—that should be obvious by now. Perhaps the voices of the more than half of us rising up in prayer and protest will help. But one thing I do know: sin grows best in the dark. Women, perhaps it is time for us to drag this humiliating truth out into the light. Perhaps it's time for us to join together and say, "Lord, have mercy on us!" I don't know, but I do know that a day is coming when all the sin of others that affects us will be washed away in pure love. But, in the meantime, let me encourage you to take Jenny's wisdom to heart. Jenny is a godly sister who has walked through fire to give you this good gift. She understands and she loves.

Elyse Fitzpatrick
Author, speaker, biblical counselor

Acknowledgments

THIS BOOK IS in your hands today because God is the God of all comfort (2 Corinthians 1:3). Throughout my life he provided mentors, professors, pastors, and friends who gently applied wisdom to my immaturities, walked with me through suffering, and encouraged my growth in Christlikeness.

To these people, my gratitude abounds:

Trish Masters, the youth group at Freeman Heights Baptist Church, and their parents, through you I saw my first glimpse of eternity—a place full of grace and familial care. You welcomed me despite my faults and gave me hope during the bleakest years of my life. Through you I vividly experienced the love of Jesus and learned to love the church.

Dr. Mark Rapinchuk, you will forever be my favorite professor because you instilled in me a love for God's inerrant word and taught each of your students the importance of reasoning well. These are two of the most priceless gifts I have ever received. I hope they are displayed in these pages.

Alex, Bethany, Erin, and Carrie, your prayers and encouragement strengthened me through this writing project.

To my first readers Andrea Lee, Ann Cherry, Ann Maree Goudzwaard, Jamie Butts, Kara Henricks, and Katie Cochran—each of you offered suggestions that made this book better.

Barbara Juliani, I am grateful that you lent your imagination to the conception of this endeavor. Your confidence spurred me on.

To Ruth Castle, Cheryl White, Alecia Sharp, Irene Stoops, and the team at New Growth Press, thank you for all the ways you contributed to this project. Many thanks to Sarah Marshall whose editorial insights and recommendations were invaluable in making this book what it is.

Nate Brooks, you are a skilled editor and a generous friend. You are also wise beyond your years, but don't tell anyone I say so!

With the deepest appreciation to Kïrsten Christianson, Joy Forrest, Darby Strickland, Jeremy Pierre, Curtis Solomon, and Greg Wilson, I recognize your individual contributions to this book. Each of you offered wisdom gained through many years of caring for suffering souls. I humbly admit that the content of appendix 1, "Porn and Abuse," is entirely beyond the scope of my knowledge or experience. Thank you for making this information available to my readers.

Curtis, my best and most resilient friend, you are my dreaming tree. You also assembled my appendices with the utmost alacrity—and I am grateful! Thank you for allowing some of the hardest lessons we have learned to comfort others. I know this vulnerability is borne out of a deep love for Jesus and a humble desire to serve his church. Your courage brings God glory and bolsters my hope.

Introduction

I WRESTLED THROUGH the process of writing this book and grappled with finding the best words to voice the hardships that come with being married to someone who struggles with sexual sin. This thought from Timothy Keller summarizes my experience well: "Sexual love—if it's not expressed in an exclusive, lifelong covenant relationship—is dehumanizing."[1] What do you think about this quote? If it rings true, this book will address some of the ways you have been degraded and dehumanized by your husband. For me, this repeated trial has often felt lonely, but the isolation of the experience stands in stark contrast to how common this struggle has become. You might feel lonely too, but you are not alone. A 2014 Barna Group Survey found that 64 percent of Christian men and 15 percent of Christian women view porn at least once a month.[2] More wives than you realize are facing this difficulty.

Yet you are not wrong for feeling degraded. When we consult the Bible, the reasons for this feeling become apparent. Let's think together about a biblical vision of marriage. This will clarify why porn has deeply corrosive effects on couples.

Marriage is supposed to point to the relationship between Christ and the church (Ephesians 5:31–32). Pornography use

1

erodes significant aspects of the picture that every husband is meant to reflect—namely Christ's steadfast and sacrificial relationship with his bride (Ephesians 5:25). When using porn, the man meant to display Christ's resolute love is selfishly accepting an invitation to enter the sexual experiences of others. Although wives are called to represent the church through wholehearted respect and submission to the leadership of their husbands (Ephesians 5:22–24), they must stand against the sinful purposes of a husband when (by his lustful imaginations) he is violating the exclusivity of marriage. In short, if pornography has impacted your marriage, the beautiful imagery set forth in Scripture has been distorted and probably seems like a distant, unattainable fairy tale.

The marriage covenant is meant to portray Christ's passionate pursuit of the church he died to redeem. Porn use makes a mockery of that covenant. Although porn involves illicit, sexual thoughts, there is more to it than mere imagination. He is willfully looking at illicit images that objectify real people and pursuing them for the sole purpose of selfish sexual gratification. These experiences are simultaneously real and phantom, brought to him by actors on a page or screen. As the continuum of unfaithfulness moves from lustful thoughts to actions, we can also see that pornography is different from an affair. It lacks the emotional connection or physical contact of an adulterous relationship, which is a mutual exchange. Yet sexual images still hold the power to wreak havoc. Over time, the deleterious effects of porn can slowly destroy a marriage.

Porn use violates all of God's intentions for marriage, but growth and healing are possible when there's repentance. As I write this, Curtis and I are in our nineteenth year of marriage. We've battled pornography many times over the years. By God's grace, we have weathered the devastating effects of porn and remain deeply committed to fighting for our marriage. We've also seen that the church isn't well-equipped to care for women whose marriages have been hurt by porn. I have long wondered why so few books have been written specifically for wives living in the aftermath of porn use. One possible reason is the embarrassment of discussing sexual sin, let alone admitting it's been a part of one's own marriage. That's another reason this wasn't an easy book to write (and I know it will be painful for you as you read it). Embarrassment aside, I think an even more weighty reason so few resources exist is the difficulty of articulating the confusion of the lived experience. Porn's effects on the heart of a spouse are hard to encapsulate in words. The aftermath of each incident across every marriage looks very different. As one who has experienced this pain firsthand, it is always a soul-wrecking experience. I've also found it to be an unpredictable experience. Each time Curtis gave way to temptation and looked at porn, I responded differently. Sometimes I was burdened by crippling sadness and felt discouraged to the point of hopelessness. Other times, anger and resentment crowded out all other emotions. Sometimes I drew close to the Lord in the aftermath of Curtis's confession. Other times I pushed away time in the Word, too frustrated, bewildered, and numb to even pray.

There are many things I hope you gain from this book, but one of my greatest hopes is that you leave this book with firmly established, genuine friendships within a local church. One woman whose husband lost his job due to porn use explained her dilemma in a helpful way. She said that after his sin was revealed, everyone was so focused on addressing him and his issues that she felt swept to the side; nobody came to her aid as she muddled through tremendous suffering. Her story is the story of so many wives. You are the living, breathing collateral damage of your husband's porn use. Have you shown anyone the shrapnel in your soul? Has anyone helped dress your wounds? So many women suffer in silence. I hope this book serves you by acknowledging some of the ways you have been injured. As you survey your heart and emotions, they may resemble a wasteland. Your sorrowful soul needs to be tended, and this can't happen unless you draw close to the Lord and learn to rely on the help of his Spirit and his church. I know I won't be able to tend to every aspect of your experience, but I hope the following pages lend you words to begin to fully articulate your story to a trusted friend or counselor who can point you toward additional resources that will help you heal.

This book won't address everything you need to know after you encounter porn in your marriage. For example, this book will discuss forgiveness and how to respond to your husband's repentance, but if you know this is (or will be) extremely difficult for you, there are other wise resources you can consult on the important topics of forgiveness and reconciliation. If you've come to this book looking for a step-by-step plan that neatly articulates a resolution to your situation, you have come to the wrong place. Every woman's situation is different, and it would be unwise to offer a one-size-fits-all approach to dealing with couples who are facing nuanced problems. Books were never meant to take the place of relationships. Only a skilled pastor or counselor will be able to enter your world in order to guide you in the most Christ-honoring direction.

This book has a different purpose. Curtis's porn use affected me differently each time he lapsed back into sinful habits, but a few things remained the same. Each time, I wished that I didn't feel so alone. Each time, I wanted to glean hope from a helpful book written by a wife who had persevered through her husband's porn use. Each time, I yearned for a friend to ask good questions, listen to my answers, and pray with me through the hardest moments. Finally, after years of praying for a book like this one and wondering why no one had written it yet, God supplied me with the courage to write it.

In the pages that follow, we will engage with various topics that have resonated with me over the course of my marriage. It is formatted to read like a hybrid between a book and a Bible study.

Come to it with your Bible in hand. You will gain the most from it that way.

Several chapters center around biblical texts—James 3:17–18, 1 Samuel 25, and Luke 7:36–50. Reviewing the related section of Scripture at the beginning of each chapter (where noted) will familiarize you with the passage and ensure that you gain as much as possible from your reading. We are going to move slowly through these texts. We will look at a host of applications and implications because in the aftermath of porn, what you most need is a safe place to tend your heart and draw near to the Lord. The focal passages I have chosen offer hope to wives of both repentant and unrepentant husbands (though some passages necessitate emphasizing one more than the other). When the heavy burden of sorrow weighs down one's soul, it is helpful to pause and lean hard on a few solid truths. So, we will carefully examine each passage from multiple angles, occasionally rewinding to look at the same chapter and discussing additional insights found in the narrative. It is my prayer that each facet will encourage your faith and refresh you during a season when you desperately need spiritual sustenance.

The topics we will explore include lamenting, resolving not to blame yourself for your husband's sin, bringing others into your struggle, obtaining the wisdom only God can give, choosing to do what you can, establishing effective accountability, refusing sinful vengeance, encountering mercy that gives hope, cultivating a welcoming heart, and growing through suffering. Throughout the book you will encounter lists of questions meant to help you examine your thoughts, emotions, motives, and actions. Take time to ponder these, then highlight and discuss the ones that are helpful to you.

If you are a husband coming to this book because your wife is struggling with porn, you are most welcome here. I apologize if the language is off-putting. I am well aware that it could be, but I ask you to please bear with me and read along. There is hope in these pages for you too.

However, this book primarily addresses wives for the following reasons:

- At the time of this writing, men are still the predominant consumers of pornography. (Yet I acknowledge that while being the "predominant" segment of users, men are not the exclusive consumers of porn. Women also struggle with sexual sin. Your pain and sorrow are equally worthy of considerate care.)
- In my limited experience as a writer, I could not find a way to use gender-neutral language while maintaining an enjoyable reading experience. The option of using inclusive language throughout felt clunky.
- Since men and women have different roles and experiences in marriage, I am writing from my experience as a married woman. I will address some concerns that are specific to women (like the issue of submission in the story of Abigail). Because there are unique aspects to the experience of men and women and how they should respond, my husband, Curtis Solomon, has written a companion book specifically for men on the topic. This book is entitled *Redeem Your Marriage: Hope for Husbands Who Have Hurt through Pornography*.

As we set out on this journey, I want to ask you to take this crucial first step: If you haven't already, it's time to ask for help. If you are intending to read this book alone, please reconsider. Fighting pornography is not something you and your spouse are equipped to handle alone—you need to let others into your pain and struggle. Chapter 4 will go into this topic further. However, I urge you not to wait until you get to that chapter—start now. This entire book is meant to be read alongside a mature, Christian friend. Sexual sin (whether it is your husband's or your own) seeks to detach individuals from the church. Sorrows and sins that remain in the dark quickly fester and spread. Eventually, untrue thoughts will grow large enough to pummel and break you. Ongoing, vulnerable conversations in the context of Christian community are a provision from God for your good. I promise that you will benefit more from this book if you delve into it honestly alongside a sister in Christ.

Whether or not you take my advice and invite someone to read this book with you (although I hope you do!), please know that you are not alone on this journey. God will be with you every step of the way.

1

Fallen Leaves

MY YARD IS home to many trees—thirty-eight at last count. They are a continual source of enjoyment for my family. At the kitchen window, I observe the seasonal changes in the Japanese maples. Each spring they reveal tiny, crumpled leaves. The first year we lived in this house I was fooled by the show and assumed a late frost had withered them just as they emerged. However, within a few days they unfurled into vibrant crimson flags. We selected the sturdiest limb from the stand of trees in the front yard to support a swing that draws kids from the neighborhood. Another massive pine tree boasts imaginary "bunk beds" where the same children gather and relax on broad branches. And branches are occasionally downed in thunderstorms, providing my husband and sons material for their beloved hobby of whittling around the firepit. God's trees give so many pleasing gifts.

There is only one time during the year that I don't enjoy our trees—autumn. Frosty temperatures send us a cascade of dead leaves—tens of thousands of them. In order to maintain a beautiful yard, each one needs to be arrested. The tedious tasks of raking, bagging, and putting them out for compost are daunting jobs. It takes several weeks, but once the job is complete, we are flooded with a sense of relief and the assurance that an entire year will pass before this difficult work must be done again.

That guarantee was always the case until last year, after a new neighbor moved in. Fall came, and like clockwork, each of our neighbors grabbed rakes, blowers, and mowers. They descended on their own yards and took their respective leaves captive. My family did the same. When we finished, we checked the leaf box for the year and congratulated ourselves on a job well done. Except this time the job wasn't actually finished. About a week later, we noticed more leaves in our yard. Our new neighbor hadn't done any raking. Several bags worth of his leaves had blown into our yard. We raked and removed the leaves, initially assuming that he hadn't yet gotten around to the job but would tend his lot soon. After several months passed and the slow, relentless trickle of leaves continued, we realized that respite from this work wasn't coming. Our neighbor indicated no resolve to dispose of his fallen leaves. Resentment began to build in us as we contemplated our new routine. Leaf raking once had defined, seasonal parameters. Yes, it was always a difficult job that required regular discipline, but now dead leaves became a daily concern requiring unrelenting vigilance. Our neighbor's lack of discipline created an ongoing problem for us too!

Suffering for the Sins of Your Husband

Porn use is infinitely graver than this battle against our neighbor's leaves. Having a husband who struggles with porn doesn't just give you some extra work to do, as our neighbor's neglect of his leaves did for us. It can shake your faith in God, destroy your sense of identity, and leave you feeling alone, confused, and hurt. In my use of this analogy, please know that I am not minimizing the seriousness of the problem you are facing. My hope is that the analogy will illuminate your experience by acknowledging certain aspects of the struggle that you might not have recognized or might have been unable to articulate. For example, virtually every person encounters sexual temptation. We all need to fight it in a disciplined way. Every person who experiences victory over sexual temptation works hard to do so. But what about the person who is disengaged from or losing the fight for purity? The dead leaves accumulate quickly, and they can't be contained by invisible property lines. Everyone who lives in close relationship with someone who views pornography is impacted by the consequences of this sin.

Your husband's porn use has left his yard littered with debris such as greed, lust, discontentment, pride, and self-indulgence. These sins are his, not yours, but they roll into your yard because you live in such close proximity. The situation becomes further complicated because you also bring sin struggles to the marriage relationship. They can quickly take on names like rage, resentment, vengeance, bitterness, discontentment, and despair. In order for your yard to be a place of beauty and flourishing, your responses will also need to be dealt with. Throughout this book, you will be asked to take an honest look at your own sin because your yard needs tending too.

If you have dealt with his porn problem for any length of time, you have probably thought to yourself something like, *Why can't he just rake his leaves? Everyone else seems to be able to manage their own sexual desires. He should get this under control right now.* You might be hoping to battle his porn use in the same way I hope to battle fall leaves. Give me fifty leaf bags, a rake, and two Saturdays. Let's sweat hard, push through the pain, and clean this mess up quickly. However, this sin is not the type of struggle that normally gets bagged up once and carted off for good. Most change is a long, slow process. It's likely that the two of you will be bagging leaves through many coming seasons, but it's worthwhile. Tending your marriage and seeing it grow over time is truly worth all the hard work it will take.

Realizing There Is Hope

As with all long, difficult endeavors, fighting pornography alongside your husband—your closest neighbor—is painful. No other challenge that I have faced has tempted me to believe the lie that I am alone. However, this is not a book solely about my experience. Through many years of ministry within the local church, my husband and I have witnessed the crippling effects of sin on God's children. We have also had the privilege of watching God's Word bring hope and change to many people, including us.

Pornography brings shame and guilt with it, which tend to isolate struggling, fearful people, but that fear doesn't have to consume your life. Your husband can change, and he might do so. Even if he doesn't, your life can abound with brave, selfless love because Jesus is a brave and selfless Savior. If you have trusted in him for salvation, then he has given you his Spirit. (1 John 4:13–16). He promises to never leave or forsake you (Hebrews 13:5). And he promises that he will complete the work of making you like himself (Philippians 1:6). So, as we sift through fragments of present brokenness, let us remember that we are kept by a Savior who loves us steadfastly.

Surveying the Landscape

The battle against porn certainly requires vigilance, but you shouldn't be the one doing all the hard work. Your spouse's leaves tend to blow across your yard sporadically. There's no guarantee what the landscape will look like—week by week or even day by day. This uncertainty is accompanied by an unending parade of tasks: Have I checked today's junk mail pile for swimsuits and lingerie? Did I bury the magazines containing questionable images far enough down in the recycling bin? Do all my internet-connected devices have secure passwords? Should I change the passwords again? How should I manage access to our streaming services? Is it even wise for our family to subscribe to streaming services? Have I unlocked my phone in front of my husband lately? Did I remember to turn the screen away from him every time I used the password to unlock it? Should I ask him if he knows my password? Would that be insulting? Does our accountability software have loopholes? Has he found and taken advantage of them?

Has his sin become something that you bear the brunt of managing? Is he serious about fighting it? Is he also working to cut off entry points? Until his pursuit of a pure heart is even more important to him than it is to you, these attempts to minimize temptation will resemble babysitting rather than teamwork toward a common goal of holiness. God has not created you to be your spouse's nanny. You are his wife. (Later in the book I will delineate the difference through a discussion of appropriate vigilance.)

The difficulty doesn't end there. Think about the prospect of discussing his sin with him. It's not an easy subject to broach. Some of these questions may have crossed your mind: Should I ask him if he's given in to the temptation to view porn lately? What if he has and he lies to me? Will I even believe his answer if I ask him about how he's doing in the area of sexual purity? If I don't think I will believe his answer, should I bother asking? If he confesses that he has been viewing porn, do I have the emotional strength to bear that right now? What if he hasn't been thinking about porn at all? Will my questions put tempting thoughts in his mind and make it harder for him to focus on holiness? Wisdom for how to handle difficult conversations will be another important topic for us to discuss later in this book.

Indifference is an equally damaging response to being repeatedly sinned against. Have you grown jaded watching the man who promised to pursue you retreat again and again into a fool's fantasy world? Does each new incident leave you feeling more discouraged? Have his lies left you believing there is no one you can trust? Does discontentment consume your heart as you evaluate your body in light of your husband's corrupt preferences? Do you consider sexual intimacy to be sorrowful or stressful, rather than joyful? Have you turned his wrong choices into excuses for your own spiritual apathy?

If any of these questions rings true, this book has much hope for you. Here you will encounter a Savior who binds up broken hearts. Here you will be invited to repent of sins you have committed in response to being sinned against.

Have you ever experienced confusion while surveying this devastation? As the wife of a person pursuing pornography, you might even feel as though you have been cheated on. Porn use is a serious breach of fidelity that deeply impacts a couple's trust and intimacy. However, we believe there are sound biblical reasons for categorizing it as something different than adultery on the spectrum of sexual infidelity. Many couples who battle pornography never broach the subject of divorce, but if you and your husband have (or if divorce is an option that you have been silently weighing), we have included appendix 3, "Is Pornography Use Grounds for Divorce?" to help answer some of your questions.

Living in Hope, Not Fear

It's incredibly hard to wait for transformation that you can't make happen. You've watched your husband struggle and witnessed the truth of John 8:33–34: sin enslaves sinners. If your husband isn't repentant and you don't see him actively pursuing holiness, you might be fearful about the future because there's no evidence to encourage you that his porn use today won't spiral into an adulterous relationship down the road. The what-ifs of your marriage can quickly become a consuming panic. Without attentiveness, fear can become your master, enslaving you much the same way that pornography holds its audience captive.

The constant threat of another porn incident is like a thunderstorm perpetually looming on the horizon. Even on a glorious, sunny spring day, it feels necessary to monitor the sky for impending storms. Do you sometimes experience dread, even in the good moments of marriage? Do you believe that it's easier to stay alert, always prepared for bad news, because it seems too crushing to be caught off guard by a new confession?

When people are unprepared to face trials, they often find their faith wavering. I have heard many thoughtful Christians say some version of this: "You are either coming out of a trial, in the midst of a trial, or getting ready to enter a trial." This well-intentioned idea takes into account the Bible's clear teaching that Christians will experience suffering. Each time I have heard this idea voiced, it came from someone who desired to prepare believers for the reality that suffering is one of the pathways God uses to make us more like Jesus (James 1:2–4). But, for someone who lives with a spouse who views pornography repeatedly, the constant threat of relapse can fuel perpetual anxiety. Viewing life as an unending cycle of trials can feel akin to having a boogeyman in the closet. Have you found yourself repeatedly dreading the moment when porn will, again, rear its ugly head? If so, then you already know how allowing your thoughts to be suspended in anxious anticipation will rob you of all the joy God extends to you through his Spirit.

A change of perspective is in order. Let's redirect the focus away from the trial. Trials are an inevitable part of every believer's journey, but they are only temporary stops along the road. Suffering is not the ultimate destination. Between now and heaven there will be trials, but we are heading for an eternity filled with unending joy. Directing attention toward the good that is coming is a better, more life-giving thought for a wife in this situation. Remember that God is working all your marital trials for your good. Therefore, God has either already worked a difficult trial for your good or is presently working difficulty for your good. And God knows how he will work all future difficulties for your good (Romans 8:28). God will continue to be faithful to you—even while your husband isn't.

Questions for Action, Discussion, and Reflection

1. Have you already found a friend who is committed to reading this book with you? If not, name a few trustworthy women and set aside time to ask for help.

2. Begin to list ways that you can regularly pray for your husband. As you interact with this book, add any new ideas that come to mind. Pray through them daily.

Further Reading on What the Bible Says about the Value of Women

Fitzpatrick, Elyse, and Eric Schumacher. *Worthy: Celebrating the Value of Women*. Minneapolis, Minnesota: Bethany House Publishers, 2020.

2
Lament

DURING AN ESPECIALLY draining season of life, I discovered information that led me to ask Curtis how he was doing in the area of sexual purity. He quickly confessed that he was struggling. This was not the first time in the battle against porn that we had cycled through this miserable scenario, but it turned out to be one of the most painful for me.

Even before he confessed his sin, circumstances felt too difficult to manage. We were both adapting to significant shifts in life. Our sleep schedule was irregular due to the demands of caring for a loved one who needed our attention all hours of the day. I was also managing a nagging health issue. On top of this, a spiritual drought brought on by many months of neglecting Scripture intake had left me spiritually brittle. When Curtis confessed his sin, my trust wasn't the only thing that shattered. My emotional well-being crumbled too. It became hard to get out of bed. Heavy grief made performing the simplest daily tasks feel like they were beyond the amount of energy I was able to exert. Deep discouragement overtook me as I surveyed the state of my soul and the state of our marriage. I really wasn't sure that I would be able to rebound from the pain or that we would be able to bridge the chasm between us.

I was barely speaking to Curtis, so I texted him: Find me a counselor.

He responded with a few names: We could go see ____ or ____?

He didn't understand my request, so I replied: I am going alone.

It's not that I didn't ever want to work together toward reconciliation—and we eventually did get wise counsel together—but as I examined my heart, I realized it resembled a war zone. I needed God's help and the help of a wise counselor to tend this sacred space. I needed to draw near to God and learn how to lament so that I could eventually learn how to hope. Robert Kellemen talks about the potential for growth out of grief. He wrote, "It's normal to hurt and necessary to grieve . . . It's possible to hope and supernatural to grow."[1]

Have you come to this book spiritually parched, grieving, and wondering, *Why can't I have a happy marriage?* I've been there. It's good to admit those things and voice your pain. You would be lying if you pretended that life is fine. Life shouldn't feel great soon after porn comes to light. This sin really does cause suffering and disconnection. You do perceive the situation rightly when you experience sadness as a result of porn; whether your spouse is forsaking you in order to secretly engage with imaginary sexual partners or you are pursuing porn as a couple, it is a violation of God's commands for purity.

Sometimes people turn to porn in an attempt to momentarily escape life's troubles, but it leads to the same disruptive end—disengagement at home. Sexual intimacy can rightfully be a place of solace for a weary spouse, but that comfort comes through mutual self-giving—a wife loving and serving her husband while the husband loves and serves his wife. Porn severs holy unity because it is primarily about an individual indulging and gratifying the flesh, even when it is indulged in together. There's no joy to be found in that self-centered, others-demeaning world. Joy comes from being loved by God and, in turn, loving God and others.

The Sorrow of Sexual Intimacy after Unfaithfulness

Porn turns the joy of sex to desolation. Those parts of your experience that have been darkened by shame need to be flooded with the light of God's Word. What are some of the sorrows you have experienced because of porn? Here's one that is especially painful: Does the togetherness of sexual intimacy feel sorrowful since his porn use has come to light? It's no wonder that there is often a deadening effect on the sexual intimacy of a couple after one or both partners view porn. In a healthy, God honoring marriage, sexual intimacy is a time of focused, loving unity, but in the aftermath of porn, the unity is fragmented and can make engaging sexually feel like the loneliest experience imaginable. Reuniting sexually with someone who has severed the exclusivity of the union is one of the most heart-wrenching experiences a spouse will ever have to face. More than that, intimacy might also become a place of embarrassment as a wife reevaluates her physical form in light of the rejection she has experienced.

You might wonder why your husband uses porn. That's a good question. There are certainly varying factors that motivate people who seek out pornography. These are worth exploring in your own marriage with the help of a counselor or pastor. When you enter these hard conversations and get down to the heart of why your husband turns to porn, you will likely find that it has everything to do with his relationship with God and little or nothing to do with you. That's why many men who view porn can honestly say they find their wives beautiful. But there's no real consolation in that affirmation because, at the core of porn use, there's still a heart of discontentment toward God and a rebellious overstepping of the boundaries he has placed on sexual expression. When we are not loving God rightly, as is always the case with porn use, it's reflected in the ways we treat our neighbors. When your husband consumes porn, he isn't loving you rightly. His unloving actions degrade intimacy, and they can damage your self-appraisal. That's why you may be tempted to feel less valuable and less beautiful after he looks at porn. If you struggled with self-image prior to marriage, his porn use will reinforce your worst thoughts about your appearance.

God intends sexual intimacy to be an exclusive gift for married couples to enjoy together. Instead, when your husband chooses to view pornography, it reinforces the powerful lies that you are dispensable and that your participation in acts of sexual intimacy is inadequate or meaningless. In most cases, husbands truly do not intend to diminish the worth of intimacy with their wives, but sin has unintended real repercussions. When he turns anywhere other than you for a sexual experience, he is acting as though you are not precious (Proverbs 5:15–23). If you've dealt with porn repeatedly, intimacy might feel increasingly humiliating. Have you found yourself wondering how long it will be before he rejects you again? Feelings of rejection and humiliation can harden into a deep-seated resentment. It's possible that the residual discouragement of your husband's ongoing or past sin has left you feeling joyless toward both the physical and emotional intimacy of marriage. Has this been your experience?

Deep Conversation with God

Porn brings with it so much pain and sorrow. What do you typically do when you feel sad? Where do you go with your pain? Do you bottle it up, refuse to feel it, or angrily vent it in the wrong places? What do you think about the idea of pouring out your grief and complaints before God? Being honest with God is something that I find very difficult. What about you—is this easy for you? Does going to God with your frustration, anger, and sadness seem like an appropriate thing to do? If not, I hope to convince you that it is.

God wants us to express the confusing spectrum of life's ups and downs in his presence. This doesn't come naturally for me. I like to wait until I have things figured out and I don't feel angry about the difficulty at hand. Once all my thoughts and emotions are in check, I go to God. But sometimes I don't go to God at all because I can't figure out the perfect way to express complicated thoughts. This is not the way I should handle problems; it's not what we see the Psalmists do. Throughout the Psalms, we see God's people going to him when they are confused, angry, and full of despair. I am slowly grasping that the times I experience those intense feelings are the times I most need to pray sincerely and reorient toward God's care for me.

A great example of this is found in Psalm 73:21–28. See how Asaph approached God in verse 22 (NIV): "I was senseless and ignorant; I was a brute beast before you." Robert Kellemen describes Asaph's honest lament this way:

> Suffering is an opportunity for God to divulge more of himself and to release more of his strength. When Asaph's heart was grieved and his spirit embittered, God brought him to his senses. Listen to his prayer. "My flesh and my heart may fail, but God is the strength of my heart and my portion forever" (Psalm 73:26). In grieving we say with Asaph, "My flesh may be scarred, my heart may be scared, but with God I can survive—forever."[2]

You might wonder whether this honest expression of pain is a contradiction to thankfulness. After all, the Bible says it's God's will for Christians to give thanks in all circumstances (1 Thessalonians 5:18). Yet, Scripture simultaneously shares many complaints from saints—over one-third of the 150 psalms are songs of lament. Laments by definition contain complaints.[3] Scripture doesn't refute itself, so how are we to reconcile the apparent discrepancy between these two responses to suffering—gratitude and complaint—which seem to counter one another? Here's the answer: There is a faithful type of prayer that voices the tension between pain and God's goodness.[4] It's called lament. Lament allows God's people to share their grievances and gratitude at the same time. This is what I hope you remember as you practice lament: We belong to a loving God who doesn't expect us to gloss over suffering. He knows we don't have everything figured out. He invites us to communicate our difficulties in real time. God welcomes us to grieve in his presence and honestly express the pain we face as a result of living in a fallen world.[5]

Just as there are two types of complaining—sinful complaints and faithful complaints—there are also sinful and faithful ways to seek consolation amid pain. Here are some examples of sinful consolations: griping to a best friend, shopping excessively, binge eating a carton of ice cream, getting drunk, bitterly replaying difficult interactions, and stewing over his sin. Can you name your own sinful consolations? These behaviors fuel self-centeredness, harden our heart toward our spouse, dampen gratitude toward God, and also make us less attune to God's good purposes in the midst of pain.

Have you submitted to the false notion that pretending everything is fine is a Christlike response? Are you trying to ignore the pain of betrayal? I know from experience that there's nothing more isolating than putting on a phony smile and speaking a sappy platitude in the face of real pain and loss. Don't tell God you are ok when you are bleeding to death. Don't smile and fake it with trustworthy friends when you are hanging on by an unraveling string.

Every trial is temporary in light of eternity, but the ways they shape our character are long lasting. God uses trials to make his children more like Jesus. Who will each of us be when we emerge from these dark tunnels? Although every person encounters pain in this life, not every person grows as a result of suffering.

Sometimes pain is the reason people give for rejecting Christianity. It's possible that this current trial could become an excuse for abandoning faith in God. The spiritual discipline of lament is marked by the desire to run toward God, rather than away from him. Do you hope to become more entrenched in your own sins or more like Jesus? If we want to grow in Christlikeness, we need to run to God and lament our pain, while at the same time committing to trusting his purposes when we can't yet see the good that he is working toward. God will come through for his people. When his children experience hardship, it is never futile. God won't let our pain go to waste. Let's resolve to be on the lookout for the good that is coming. Through lament, we can continually remind ourselves to do just that.

The Blessings of Lament

Because lament expresses both sorrow and trust, practicing it will bless us in many ways.[6] First, as with other types of prayer, it brings us into the presence of God. Second, lament encourages us to process pain faithfully. Third, lament keeps us from straying as we turn back toward God. In addition, lament also celebrates our need for God's help.[7]

Has your husband's porn use led you to the assumption that you should rely solely on yourself? Your spouse has certainly exhibited unreliability. You can't always count on him to exhibit sexual fidelity, which is the opposite of what he vowed when you married him. A lack of self-control in one area usually bleeds into other parts of life. So there may be a variety of ways he lacks dependability and self-control (e.g. skipping time with the Lord, procrastinating, regularly sleeping past his alarm, overeating, overconsuming alcohol, binge-watching TV, excessively playing video games, spending financial resources irresponsibly, manifesting a poor work ethic, lacking follow-through in other relationships, etc.). Lament is a time to remember to rely on our Heavenly Father. He loves us, has the power to meet all our needs, and always follows through with his promises. Lament says, "God, you are reliable—even when I am failed by the person in my life I had most hoped I could depend on."

How to Lament

Scripture's description of Christ reminds us that our laments will fall on sympathetic ears. Jesus is a man acquainted with grief (Isaiah 53:3). There's no need to minimize suffering and sorrow when we talk with him. If you are new to the practice of lament, here are some prompts, along with a sample prayer (in italics) to help get you started:[8]

1. Begin by pouring out anguish over your husband's sin. (Answer these questions before the Lord: What am I most sad about? What have I lost?) *Jesus, my heart is broken because my husband has betrayed, rejected, and deceived me. . . .*
2. Next, ask for God's help. (What do you need right now?) *I need your help to treat him with kindness. Only you can convict him of sin. Please help him to think about his porn use the way that you think about it. Bring him swiftly to repentance. . . .*
3. Now express hope. (Use your imagination to envision what God could do in your marriage. What do you hope your marriage will become?) *Nothing is impossible with you, Lord! Give my husband a pure heart. Provide me the grace to fully forgive. Make our marriage a testimony that brings comfort to other hurting couples. . . .*
4. Finally, take time to express trust in God, rather than the circumstances of a great marriage. (Are you willing to follow God regardless of your husband's choices? Tell him your answer.) *I don't know how this is all going to work out, but I know you are good and that you love me. I trust you to care for me perfectly, no matter what tomorrow brings. Amen."*

There are many ways to enter the practice of lament. Below there are a few to consider. As you explore them, you may find that some are more meaningful to you than others. Poetry is the medium where I can best wrestle with difficult circumstances and pour out my concerns to God. I wrote this poem of lament during a time when I was aching from the pain caused by my husband's pornography use:

Hurricane

A storm passed through our covenant.
It threatened to unbind, loose, fray the union.
The skies sunny, cleanup begins—
new construction on scarred, sacred land.
Slow progress, blistering labor.
The old, familiar landscape transfigured,
recreated by the storm (or by He who the winds obey)—
 depending on how you look (or Who you believe).

There's no hope for things to be the same
no man can step into the same trial twice;
to turn the other cheek is to move forward
 while the waters of time rush past.

These currents sweep away what could have been
as they usher in what can be—
possibilities awash with mercy.
The Keeper of rain unleashes torrents, bids them cease,
gives rain to the just and the damned.
Two of the same—the only difference is grace.
By it we are remade
washed clean.

Journaling is also a helpful pathway to lament. If you are in the habit of documenting your journey this way, take time at the end of each entry to read over your reflections, and then bring those feelings, thoughts, and situations to God in prayer. Singing your sadness is another way to approach God in lament. You can write your own lyrics or sing some written by others that express the depths of your heart. If you are a visual artist, praying while drawing or painting images that reflect your emotions is a beautiful way to approach God with your sorrow.

During some of the most difficult moments of marriage, getting spiritual food was the last thing I felt like doing. If your daily practice of reading Scripture has gone out the window, praying through psalms of lament is a way to grieve while simultaneously taking in the nourishment of God's word. Some psalms were written to be sung corporately, and others were written for individuals. Below I have listed several individual psalms of lament. You can certainly use corporate psalms in your personal time with the Lord, but I selected these because they easily flow from one who is engaged in private worship. Beside each I briefly summarized a theme relevant to our common experiences of suffering. To use this list devotionally, first read through the summaries, choose one that resonates with you today, and then read once through that psalm. Notice if there are ways your heart echoes the groaning of the psalmist. Read with a highlighter in hand, marking any phrase that describes your situation or emotional state, encourage you, or resonate strongly with you. When you are finished, reread it one more time (aloud if possible) as your own personal prayer of lament.

Psalm 4: A lament to read at bedtime.
Psalm 5: A lament to read in the morning.
Psalm 13: A lament for days when it feels like this trial will never end.
Psalm 25: A lament for when shame seeks to overtake you.
Psalm 28: A lament asking God to hear your cries and carry you.
Psalm 31: A lament during times of distress.
Psalm 43: A lament asking for God's light and truth.
Psalm 56: A lament for sadness and fear.

Psalm 57: A lament to help you remember that God is
  steadfast.
Psalm 64: A lament for days you dread an enemy.
Psalm 70: A lament for times you are poor and needy.
Psalm 71: A lament for after you've run out of strength.
Psalm 77: A lament to help you remember God's past
  faithfulness.
Psalm 86: A lament that recalls God's goodness and
  forgiveness.
Psalm 88: A lament for after you've been deserted by a
  beloved companion.
Psalm 139: A lament remembering that your unique body is
  precious to God.

Lament isn't a one-time practice. It's something that Christians can return to over and over as life unfolds new difficulties or reminds us of old ones. I want to invite you to return to this chapter as often as needed throughout the course of this book and in the years to come. Keep returning to God in your pain. Keep nourishing yourself with his word. Keep honestly expressing your heartache and dependence on your Heavenly Father. He hears you, sees you, and loves you. He is near you in your brokenness: "For thus says the One who is high and lifted up, who inhabits eternity, whose name is Holy: 'I dwell in the high and holy place, and also with him who is of a contrite and lowly spirit, to revive the spirit of the lowly, and to revive the heart of the contrite'" (Isaiah 57:15).[9]

Questions for Action, Discussion and Reflection

1. Share your current emotional state and some of the specific ways you typically process the grief you are experiencing.

2. Are there ways you have recently been disengaged and withdrawn from God? Why do you think this has been the case?

3. Has lament been a practice in your life up to this point? How will you incorporate lament in your life now?

4. There are several ways to approach the Lord in lament. Which is most appealing to you? Can you think of others that aren't listed?

5. Use one of these mediums to create your own lament.

Further Reading on Grief

Kellemen, Bob. *Grief: Walking with Jesus.* Phillipsburg, NJ: P&R Publishing, 2018.

Kellemen, Robert W. *God's Healing for Life's Losses: How to Find Hope When You're Hurting.* Winona Lake, IN: BMH Books, 2010.

Further Reading on Lament

Vroegop, Mark. *Dark Clouds, Deep Mercy: Discovering the Grace of Lament.* Wheaton, IL: Crossway, 2019.

3

Don't Blame Yourself for His Sin

IF YOU WERE around during the early days of social media, you might remember a crowdsourcing game called "Hot or Not." In case you missed it (and hopefully you did), here's a rough sketch of how "Hot or Not" was played: First, participants would upload a single photo. Then, based on this picture, users ranked the person's level of perceived attractiveness on a scale of 1 to 10. This left each player with a score reflecting the average of everyone who weighed in on his or her profile picture. (Let me say up front that I never played. Games like this are unhealthy; they feed off insecurity and self-promotion. Also, I have absolutely no desire to know whether random people on the internet find me attractive.)

Even though I disdained this game, I felt like I was playing it at home. When my husband consumed porn, it felt like being trapped in a game of "Hot or Not" that I didn't want to play. Although my husband has consistently praised me for being attractive—not only physically, but also spiritually and intellectually—his struggle with porn sent another message. With his words he was giving me an attractiveness score of ten, but when he viewed porn it felt like he was silently giving me a second score of zero.

I didn't have the words back then to share how I felt about this, but looking back I can now see how I handled it. Initially I struggled hard to reconcile these two contradictory scores. At first I gave myself the average score. *He probably really thinks that I am a mediocre five.* But as his struggle with porn persisted over years, eventually I doubted that he found me attractive at all. At some point I silently decided this must be one of the reasons he kept returning to porn. For a time I fell for one of the big lies pornography tempts us to believe—if I were better looking, my husband wouldn't turn to porn. In all this confusion, I stopped my ears to his compliments, and without ever expressing it to anyone else, I took on the number that his actions seemed to relay. I was too discouraged to fight the lies that assaulted me. Taking the zero score felt less stressful than trying to piece together the incoherent realities in our marriage.

Looking back, I can see that accepting this lie wasn't good for me or my marriage. My body wasn't to blame for my husband's porn problem. Yours isn't either. Your husband's sin is never your fault. That's the most important thing I want you to grasp from this chapter.

Body image is only one of the areas that we will be tempted to believe the lie that somehow (in some way) we are (at least partially) responsible for our husband's porn use. There is a terrible trio of lies that tempt us to take responsibility for our husband's sin, including the lie that your lack of vigilance and lack of discernment are the cause of his problem; the temptation to believe that giving him more sex, "better" sex, might remedy his porn problem; and the lie that he turns to porn because your body is not good enough. All three of these lies are completely and totally false. He is 100 percent responsible for all of his sin; none of it is your fault. Let's look more closely at these lies that may currently tempt you or could arise to tempt you in the future. Then let's look at truth that can help us disarm them.

Lie # 1: My vigilance and discernment can fix his porn problem.

Do you struggle with control issues? When you discovered that your husband was viewing porn, did you ever berate yourself for not checking the mail, not implementing the best media filters, not keeping all the screens in public areas? Did you feel like you had somehow dropped the ball? If so, it's wise to learn from past porn occurrences and make adjustments to the safeguards, but it's not going to be possible to perfectly control your husband's access. There will always be another loophole. If he really wants porn, he will get it. Your good desire to support your husband's sexual purity can easily become inappropriate surveillance.

As with every other area of life, your motives are very important. If you find yourself scrutinizing every move your spouse makes, waiting to see if he backslides then you have moved into unhelpful supervision. You are a wife, not a detective. However, if there's been any level of deception on his part, it's understandable that you occasionally find it necessary to fact-check your husband's words. That's a repercussion of his sin. Has your husband ever lied to you about porn or anything else? He probably has because "lies are the backbone that support an act of betrayal."[1]

I want to alleviate any undue pressure you feel regarding his duplicity. It's good to ask poignant questions when your spouse's actions don't seem to square with reality. By doing so you are giving him a chance to bring indiscretions into the light. That's a loving act. But there's no perfect question that will draw truth out of a heart that is intent upon deception. God doesn't expect us to detect every lie. In fact, it is guaranteed that we won't know everything, because only God is all-knowing. Despite your best efforts at discernment, you might still be deceived by your husband's lies. You are not spiritually liable for his deception at any point. If you have put your faith in Jesus, you can rest in his ability to always discern truth perfectly. Jesus won't ever be fooled by your husband's lies.

If you have been hoodwinked by your husband in the past, you are probably wondering if it will be possible to spot true repentance. Repentance starts with confession then demonstrates its genuineness through attitudes and actions (see Luke 3:8). You might feel burdened to make sure that he is genuinely turning away from entrenched, unholy habits. While sin certainly can be hidden from fallible humans (at least for a while), we'll look later at a passage in Luke that teaches humility and worship are recognizable attributes.

In the days to come, it will be impossible to accurately determine that your husband is not sinning. There is a good chance that, through practice, he has become adept at covering his tracks. For this reason, many have offered the advice "Don't police your husband." If your husband is insistent on devious pursuits, your best investigative efforts will result in him finding alternative, covert ways to gratify his cravings. Instead of policing his actions, a wise response is to pray for the fruits of repentance. Pray that any remaining hidden sin would be brought to light. Pray that rather than seeking loopholes, he will seek help from others. Pray that he will pursue Christ with the same determination that he once used to feed sinful appetites.

Only the Spirit can raise people to new life and enable them to "seek the things that are above" (Colossians 3:1). Colossians 3:9–10 says this about deception: "Do not lie to one another, seeing that you have put off the old self with its practices and have put on the new self, which is being renewed in knowledge after the image of its creator." Using porn is the opposite of the progression these verses describe. It's no surprise that pornography, masturbation, and lying often go hand in hand. The act of watching porn is caving in to the old self. Just as truth-telling is an indication of putting on the new self, lying indicates that a person is gratifying the flesh. Honesty is the fruit of a contrite heart. If your husband is unrepentant, he will most likely conceal his sexual sin. Once he repents, he will confess his transgressions.

While your spouse is consuming pornography, you might also be tempted to lie for him. Any past deception on your part also needs to be confessed and repented of. Have you covered for your husband or made it easier for him to hide his sexual sin? If you want to remain faithful to Christ, this is not an option. Lying could temporarily delay consequences so you might convince yourself that you are protecting your husband, your family, your church, your livelihood, your family's reputation, or the perceived integrity of his ministry. If you help weave a safety net of lies, you are creating an environment in which your husband's sin can continue to grow unfettered. Heed this warning: "Bread gained by deceit is sweet to the man, but afterward his mouth will be full of gravel" (Proverbs 20:17). You belong to a merciful God. Even if you experience repercussions from the consequences of your husband's sin, they will be used for your good. Taking matters into your own hands and covering up his sin will only lead to worse consequences down the road. (If your husband is serving the local church in any capacity, appendix 2, "Ministry after Porn," will answer more of your questions.)

In the next chapter, we will talk about how to wisely let others into your story. Your husband may be unhappy with your decision to disclose his sin to others (even though it is for his benefit), but it's also possible that he could be relieved or spurred on to new growth. Regardless of his response, you can rest in the assurance of Proverbs 12:22: "Lying lips are an abomination to the LORD, but those who act faithfully are his delight." Have you come to a point where the thought of delighting God sounds better than anything else? God loves his children's obedience. Obeying God is better than making your husband happy. It is better than financial security. It's better than the social currency that comes from having a glowing reputation. Pray that God will embolden you to speak the truth, even if it is costly.

If the goal isn't to control your husband's sinful behavior, what can you hope to attain instead? The best goal moving forward is reliance on our all-powerful God. You cannot be everywhere at once, but God is. You cannot discern your husband's thoughts, but God knows all of them. You are not God; therefore, it will never be possible for you to know or see everything. Have you acknowledged God's sovereignty by accepting your limitations as a wife?

While you can't micromanage him to purity, his porn problem still necessitates employing vigilance. But if vigilance isn't going to fix his porn problem, what is the purpose? Vigilance is a loving form of awareness that looks for ways to ease his struggle. Surveillance is often motivated by a heart of anger and retribution, a desire for control, or a heart filled with fear. Appropriate vigilance comes from a desire to be faithful to God. It is also the product of a hopeful heart, because true love always hopes (1 Corinthians 13:7). True love expresses a genuine desire that your husband will one day gain victory over his sin. God tells us to bear one another's burdens (Galatians 6:1–2). Love says, "You are carrying a heavy load. There are four shoulders in this marriage—let me share some of the weight of your struggle with you."

As you seek to help, please remember that your earnest care cannot sanctify your husband. Only the Holy Spirit can change a heart. You are not responsible for making him holy. You are called to walk alongside him in wise ways, seeking to lessen his temptation when possible. Your husband doesn't need to be controlled by you; he needs the conviction that only the Spirit can bring. Pray that the Holy Spirit will fill your husband's life with the types of good fruit that crowd out any remaining desire for porn. Pray fervently for love, faithfulness, and self-control to develop in his life.

Lie #2: I can fix his porn problem with sex.

Does sex seem like an onerous duty you must fulfill in order to keep your husband from sinning? Have you ever thought that if you offered your husband more sex, he wouldn't be tempted? One of the reasons you might believe this is because this harmful message has been conveyed by more than one popular Christian marriage resource. A chapter in *The Great Sex Rescue* entitled "Your Spouse Is Not Your Methadone" says this: "...*Every Man's Battle* tells wives, 'When men aren't getting regular sexual release, their eyes are more difficult to control. Help him out in this battle. Give him release.' Instead of seeing sex as a holistic experience that is passionate, pure, and personal, sex becomes about meeting his quota for climaxes."[2]

If you've swallowed the lie that sex is about you giving him "release" so that he doesn't turn to porn, please hear this—*this wrong way of thinking objectifies wives.* You are not a means to an end. You are a person with indelible dignity who deserves to be treated with care and tenderness. God imbues the sexual experience with good purposes—giving and receiving mutual pleasure, procreating, and bonding a husband and wife into a one-flesh union. God said that it is not good for man to be alone. Sex is one of the ways he unites husbands and wives. The closeness and joy of sexual intimacy within marriage is a vivid expression of this togetherness. Sex isn't intended to be something you do to him to pacify his sexual urges; it's supposed to be something you joyfully experience together.

Your husband's rebellion against God's purposes for sex puts you in a uniquely painful position because you are the only one he is supposed to experience sexual intimacy with. His rejection is first and foremost an affront to God. It is also a slap in your face. When your husband pursues porn, he's seeking a fantasy that will always evade his grasp. He is pining away for a new, exciting experience, but novelty is fleeting. As soon as you have it—you don't have it anymore. In addition to this, his hunger for sexual experience is disproportionate. It is completely out of step with God's intentions for sexual expression. David Powlison articulates well the holy pleasure of sex, rightly experienced:

Sex thrives in a context of marital commitment, safety, trust, affection, giving, closeness, intimacy, and generosity. It flourishes as a normal form of love within marriage . . . Sex with your spouse can be simple and self-giving, freely given and freely received. Sexual interactions can express honesty, laughter, play, prayer, and ecstasy.[3]

That's a good goal to aim towards, but it won't be attainable while your husband is fighting against God's intentions. If your sex life is in shambles, it's not because you haven't given your husband enough or good enough sex, it's because he has rebelled against God and mistreated you in the process.

Have you ever viewed pornography for "educational" reasons in hopes of learning how to give your husband "better" sex? Has your unrepentant and selfishly misguided husband pressured you to watch porn so that you can "learn" from it? Here's what you'll have to remember to fight these temptations: Gazing at a computer screen in hopes of partaking in or preparing to have a fulfilling sexual experience is futile. Porn can't ever build the healthy intimacy we long for.

God created us to experience real relationships full of meaningful connections. All of the other ways we build intimacy—praying together, singing, conversing, laughing, sharing a meal, taking a walk, hugging, enjoying a hobby together, and working toward a common goal (to name a few)—can be experienced across a wide array of friendships and familial relationships, but sexual connection is exclusive. It has been reserved by God solely for a wife and her own husband. This doesn't make sex a better or more important way to connect, but it does mean that its boundaries must be respected. And, when those boundaries aren't respected, relational consequences will fall at the feet of the sinner, not the one who is being sinned against. Your husband doesn't need you to pick up some new sex tips in order to have better sex. He needs to repent of his unholy views of sex and learn to rejoice in and be satisfied with the wife God has given him (Proverbs 5:18). Authors Gregoire, Lindenbach, and Sawatsky talk about this in an insightful way:

> You can't defeat porn by simply having a husband transfer his lust and objectification to a "safe" source—his wife. You defeat porn by rejecting the kingdom of darkness view of sex, that it is only about taking and using someone to meet your needs, and adopting a kingdom of heaven view of sex: that it's about a mutual, passionate knowing and sacrificial serving. God never meant for women to be men's sexual methadone.[4]

If your sex life is broken, God can certainly heal it. But your husband will have to take the first steps (and then many subsequent steps) in the process. He will have to repent of the ways he has sinned against God and against you through his porn use. It will likely be a very gradual healing over time that comes as your husband demonstrates his repentance by exercising tenderness, patience, and self-control and as you slowly, incrementally extend trust to him.

Lie #3: My body is part of the problem.

Body image issues often arise (or intensify) in women whose husbands use porn. Most people don't have the physique of a supermodel. Airbrushed or not, most bodies will never be the type that could appear in a lingerie ad. But when your husband chases fantasies featuring women with those faces and bodies, his actions are relaying an untrue message—that you need to become someone different (or perhaps a more physically attractive version of who God made you) in order to satisfy his longings. Don't believe that message—it's a lie.

Temptation is heightened because your husband's voice is one of many in a chorus of off-key voices in this hypersexual, image-focused culture. A one-dimensional vision of womanhood is perpetually pushed on us. This off-kilter understanding claims that your façade is more important than your substance. If you are like me, all these untrue voices have probably taken a toll on you. The remainder of this chapter will invite you to explore your attitude toward the unique body that God lovingly crafted for you, then behold our embodied savior, and finally, look to the Spirit who is pleased to dwell within those who belong to Jesus.

My struggle with body image didn't start because of my husband's porn problem, but that has been an exacerbating factor in my frustration with my body. Many times over the years I have mentally criticized my weight and set unrealistic goals to become more fit, rather than thanking God that I am generally strong and healthy. Can you relate? When you see your reflection in the mirror, do you express gratitude to God for the frame that he's given you, or do you feel combative toward it? It's not surprising that warped body image emerges amidst a cacophony of voices that send inaccurate messages about the true worth of every human frame. And it's especially hard to stay attuned to God's good purposes when your spouse consumes porn. It can become a constant battle to remember that external beauty is not the highest beauty that exists.

Have you ever imagined that if you could attain the airbrushed version of yourself, maybe your husband wouldn't struggle with porn anymore? If you dropped the extra pounds and toned all the muscles, then he would finally be able to appreciate you fully. Don't fall for that lie. Your appearance isn't the cause of your husband's sin. Your attempts at a makeover could never change his heart. Women who try to compete with paid models are buying into an ineffectual solution. God does not want wives to strive to fulfill the sinful sexual fantasies of their husbands;

instead, God intends to transform your husband's desires so that he understands godly character is more attractive than any physical attribute.

Sharing my thoughts and struggles with trusted Christian friends has been one of the ways God has helped me navigate this issue. Even as I prepared to write this chapter, an encouraging phone conversation with my friend Andrea Lee was pivotal in helping me clarify these particular thoughts. As you consider these ideas and discuss them with a wise friend, I pray the same will be true for you.

We should care for our bodies well, but it is important to do it for the right reasons. Maintaining a healthy lifestyle is wise. This important aspect of stewardship can and should be a joyful experience. Exercising regularly, sleeping adequately, eating healthily, setting aside time for fun and refreshment, and maintaining a weight that you and your doctor agree is appropriate for you are holy endeavors. When you steward your body well, you will have more energy to enjoy and serve God, your family, and the church. God is honored when you seek to eat and drink and do all things for His glory (1 Corinthians 10:31). God is not honored when you mistreat your body by obsessively monitoring calories, exercising to exhaustion, binge eating, or squandering precious time scrutinizing yourself in the mirror and wondering if you could fix your husband's porn problem by becoming prettier. Nor is God honored when you reach a point of deep despair or calculated revenge and cease to spend time caring for your body because your husband has rejected you physically.

We express care for our bodies by resisting combative thoughts or actions against the frames God has given us and also by learning to live purposefully within our bodies. I am still in the process of learning to do this, but I know with certainty that you and I won't experience contentment or peace while striving for physical perfection. That improperly oriented motivation will need to be directed toward something better and certainly attainable. Ephesians 2:8–10 describes the better motivation: "For by grace you have been saved through faith. And this is not your own doing; it is the gift of God, not a result of works, so that no one may boast. For we are his workmanship, created in Christ Jesus for good works, which God prepared beforehand, that we should walk in them."

Through the work of Jesus on the cross, God delivers his children from death (and vain striving) into purposeful living. Seeking the elusive, perfect body will distract you from a truly satisfying life. God lovingly, intentionally crafted your body. Your unique frame is well-suited for his purposes. His plan for you is attainable. It includes good works that he imagined in advance. Isn't it astounding that the God who created the entire universe took time to plan specific acts of worshipful service that you alone were crafted to complete? God never second-guesses your worth and dignity. He does all things well, including making you!

You are stamped with God's image, but his image in you has been marred by sin. In contrast, Jesus is a perfect representation. Scripture says he is the exact imprint of God (Hebrews 1:3). He's the one sinless representation of God's image. Jesus is God embodied. So when we think about what it means to live life in a body, he is our only perfect example.

Before Jesus was born, Isaiah accurately described his appearance. Essentially, God gave one of his prophets Jesus's rating—"Hot or Not"—and then made sure it would be recorded for subsequent generations. Before you read this prophecy, what do you think Isaiah recorded? Can you guess Jesus's score?

Here's the verse that helps us imagine what our Savior looked like when he walked the earth over 2,000 years ago: "[Jesus] had no form or majesty that we should look at him, and no beauty that we should desire him" (Isaiah 53:2). God, who took on human skin, is described by inerrant Scripture as average looking. Isaiah clearly isn't trying to flatter our Savior. He says that Jesus's face and body were not notably attractive. Jesus came to this earth absolutely perfect and not especially handsome. What does this tell us about the priorities of our loving, wise Father? Why do you think God wanted us to know this information about our Messiah? In what ways does this truth contradict inaccurate notions of physical perfection?

Image-driven culture leaves its mark, and there's a nagging part of me that doesn't want Isaiah's assessment to be true. Why do I find myself imagining a savior with perfect teeth, thick glossy hair, and chiseled arms? I mistakenly equate perfection with handsomeness because my perceptions and priorities have been broken by sin, and, as a result, I have misplaced a fundamental truth about embodiment: Jesus didn't put on flesh to be our homecoming king. Sexiness isn't a fruit of the spirit. Jesus wasn't concerned about looking good because he came in human form to love, serve, and save us.

God's priority for me is that I become like Jesus by loving and serving others. God has given me a body so that I can enjoy, worship, and adore him with it. Those are the things my body was made for. The delight that comes from being an embodied creature isn't accessed by making me the center of a kingdom that adores my beauty. Embodiment is wonderful because God imagined each person's unique frame and also spoke a world into existence that is suited to nourish, sustain, and astound embodied beings. Embodiment gives us eyes to see God's glory expressed in creation and hearts to trust him by faith. The wonder of embodiment culminates in the gospel. You exist in a world made by God who knows you intimately and loves you so much that he provided a way for you to abide with him forever, even though you have spit in his face out of the very lips he crafted. Embodiment doesn't magnify your greatness. It gives you an opportunity to know and worship the one majestic and great God with all your heart, mind, soul, and strength. Embodiment means you have hands and feet to love your neighbors as yourself.

When we behold Jesus, we won't find handsomeness. We will be astonished by his perfect beauty because he embodies perfect love. And as you draw near to him, you also will be transformed by his love for you. This supernatural transformation is called sanctification, and it happens because the Holy Spirit lives inside each and every Christian. God values your body so much that he sent his Spirit to live within it. This is called indwelling, and it is yet another astounding outworking of the gospel that is manifest within our physical bodies. Remembering the indwelling of the Holy Spirit is important for both you and your husband—for him as he fights porn and for you as you combat any body image distortion you've experienced. Lainey Greer describes this truth beautifully:

> Paul sought (in 1 Corinthians 6:19) to provide the Corinthians with ample evidence of a higher calling on their bodies than mere physical, temporal pleasures. Their bodies were marked out for much greater purposes, one of those being sanctification. Sanctification occurs by the Spirit who indwells embodied believers to impart his fruits of holy living. Embodiment is significant in the Spirit's role, as sanctification finds expression through the body. His presence supplied to the Christian becomes the enabling power to physically live out the command to glorify God.[5]

Jesus is perfectly beautiful. He also perfectly empowers us, by his Spirit, to become beautiful.

And that's not the only good news! Jesus is also full of compassion as we wrestle with suffering and sin surrounding body image. It truly does hurt to be rejected by a spouse. We can go to Jesus with that pain. He knows what it is like to live life in a normal body. While he walked this earth, he endured unimaginable rejection. After Isaiah describes Jesus's physical appearance, he says this: "He was despised and rejected by men; a man of sorrows, and acquainted with grief; and as one from whom men hide their faces he was despised, and we esteemed him not" (Isaiah 53:3). As you face the impact of your husband's sin, you have a Savior who understands. You have encountered tremendous rejection, but Jesus has experienced much more. His kindness toward you abounds. His attentive care will rest on you while you wait for him to save or sanctify your spouse.

So as you come before the Lord with your sorrow, grief, and rejection, remind yourself of this truth: neither the culture you live in nor your husband's estimation of your frame is the plumb line. God created you. Only he has the right to define your purpose and estimate your value. If your spouse looks at porn, he is choosing garbage. Porn will always be ugly, cheap, and worthless in the eyes of God. Your husband could look at every bit of porn in the world, and not one of those encounters will please God. And not one of those encounters is your fault. Your God is pleased with the way he designed your unique frame. Rest in his affirmation. Allow it to become your own. When you regard your body, ask God to give you gratitude and peace. Ask him to remind you that you are indwelled by his spirit, equipped for good works, and loved by a compassionate, beautiful Savior. And ask him to remind you that his thoughts about you and his purposes for your body are ultimate—the highest, truest, and most beautiful reality.

Questions for Action, Discussion, and Reflection

1. Have there been times when your attempts at appropriate vigilance have become controlling surveillance? Name a few specific ways that this chapter can help you respond more wisely to your husband's sin?

2. Have you attempted to fix your husband's porn problem through more or "better" sex? What will you say to yourself next time this temptation arises?

3. Have you ever viewed porn thinking that it might help your sex life? If so, how will you fight that temptation in the future?

4. Name a few of the good works that God has uniquely suited you to carry out. Ask him to open your eyes to new opportunities to serve him.

5. Have you felt ashamed of your body since the revelation of your husband's porn use? If yes, in what ways?

6. When you look in the mirror, do you ever figuratively wage war on your body by thinking untrue or unrealistic thoughts about the way it "should" look? Make a list of negative thoughts you think about yourself. Discuss aspects of this chapter that can reframe your thinking.

7. Do you ever wage war on your body by starving, binge eating, purging, exercising to exhaustion, or participating in any other destructive habits? If yes, eating disorders are dangerous (and at times even deadly). Please don't delay sharing your struggle with your doctor and a counselor so that they can assist you in getting help.

8. Do you take time to care for your body through rest, exercise, and nutritious food? Is your motivation for self-care a desire to honor God with your body, or something else? Share your current self-care practices and motivations, along with ways that you would like to grow in any area.

Further Reading on Eating Disorders
Dunham, David and Krista. *Table for Two: Biblical Counsel for Eating Disorders*. Greensboro, NC: New Growth Press, 2021.

Further Reading on Theology of the Human Body
Allison, Gregg R. *Embodied: Living as Whole People in a Fractured World*. Grand Rapids, MI: Baker Books, 2021.

4

Let Others In

I BECAME A Christian around age fifteen. Leading up to my salvation, several friends from school invited me to their youth group. My initial visit to Freeman Heights Baptist Church was life changing. I was riveted to my seat from the moment my youth minister opened the Bible and began to teach us the gospel. I came away with newly granted desires to seek God and understand his Word. After that first night, I started counting down the days each week until the next Wednesday.

A short time later, my parents separated. This decision came as a complete surprise to me. The sequence and timing of these two events are conspicuous reminders of God's sovereign care for me. God grabbed hold of me just before one of the most heartbreaking seasons of my life. My parents eventually divorced. So, the rest of high school was marked by upheaval, uncertainty, and painful changes at home. Had God not given me himself and his church as steady anchors during that storm, I don't know where I would be today.

Life at home was sad. Wednesday night youth group became a reprieve. It was the highlight of every week. My new church quickly embraced me as one of their own. Several girls from youth group became my closest friends. Their families showered me with care—inviting me on family vacations, welcoming me to the table for family dinners, and making guest bedrooms available anytime I needed to stay. Although I was never in physical danger at home, I was in danger of losing sight of God's goodness or seeking relief for my pain outside of him. My welcoming friends helped me remember God's constant care.

Rachel was one of my best friends. Today she serves the church as a pastor's wife. She is also a gifted musician. Thanks to her mom's affectionate hospitality during my high school years, I ate many meals and slept many nights in their home. Over the years, Rachel introduced me to great music. She also patiently endured my off-key (yet joyful) vocals. At her house I awoke most mornings to the best sort of alarm clock—the sound of piano practice. I can still hear the sound of Rachel singing "Hold Me Jesus" by Rich Mullins. If you've never heard it, please take a moment to look up the lyrics or listen now.

This song resonated with me then because the relationships and routines that had once been reliable safety nets were coming undone. It reminded me that through all the pain, Jesus was surely holding on to me. The lyrics recalled God's presence in my life, which I envisioned being like a warm hug. God is near his children when their hearts are broken (Psalm 34:18). Jesus, my Savior, and his people, the church, comforted me when I was a scared teenage girl. Jesus makes all these comforts available to you too. Second only to Jesus, the church can become your biggest ally through life's struggles—no matter what you are facing.

The revelation of your spouse's sexual sin may be new, or this might be a recurring sin you have fought for years. Maybe he is already demonstrating repentance. Maybe you recently stumbled upon the first incriminating piece of evidence and are trying to figure out a way forward. In each case, questions might arise in your mind: *Do I have the right to insist that he seeks counseling/accountability? At what point does sharing his sin with others become gossip? Should I contact my pastor or community group leader? My husband is the pastor. Who can I turn to for help?* In the days to come, other pressing questions could come to mind. Remember in chapter one when I encouraged you to enlist the help of a friend? Now I would like to ask you to also bring a pastor and a counselor into your story. As you are helping bear your husband's burdens, God has provided his church to simultaneously bear yours. You need a safe place to ask hard questions.

Unasked questions can lead to settled discouragement and despair. Write down questions as they come to mind. Take them before the Lord in prayer and take them to Scripture. Then take them to the friend who is reading this book alongside you. She will be able to help you determine where to go to find answers—your pastor, community group leader, counselor, and accountability partner could all be helpful resources. Be patient and persistent. Some questions take time to answer. Some questions cannot be answered this side of eternity. The same God who welcomes our lament will not turn away a faith-filled, questioning heart. Later in this chapter there's a list of questions for you to think through and address with your pastor and counselor. Today is not the right moment to take all the questions you have to your husband and demand answers. Some of your most important questions will be best asked and answered down the road, in the presence of a counselor. Right now I am only asking you to begin the intentional practice of writing down your questions so that in time they can be addressed in the appropriate context.

Scripture makes it clear that sin cannot be overcome without confession. At the same time, Scripture takes a firm stance against gossip. Gossip spreads information without seeking to love the person being talked about. One particularly damaging form of gossip is venting. You will need to talk through this situation, but discussion should be strictly limited to beneficial confidants. These are people who will help you work toward God-honoring responses. You might be tempted to unload this burden on your best/closest friend(s). After all, that's what friends are for, right? Not necessarily. Your closest friends are not always the best support system in this scenario. They could be predisposed to blindly take your side and advocate for your rights in a way that is unfruitful. If the person you share your husband's sin with begins to give unbiblical advice, pushes for an immediate divorce, encourages you toward vengeance, or speaks ill of your husband, then this person is not a source of godly counsel and consulting him or her further is gossip.

As you prayerfully consider who to confide in, the goal is to involve spiritually mature people who will love, shepherd, encourage, rebuke, and, if necessary, facilitate church discipline for his good. You will most likely end up enlisting additional support along the way, but a good starting point is to call your pastor, counseling pastor, or community group leader and set up a time to meet. If you'd like, bring the friend who is reading this book with you to the first meeting.

Gathering the best people to provide you care and counsel is not always easy. You may have already tried earnestly and failed to find people who are able to help. Divulging deep brokenness and then receiving no help can be very, very disheartening, but please don't give up. Keep trying until you get the help you need. Call your pastor today. If he is shepherding his flock well, he will either offer good counsel or readily refer you to a counselor or mature Christian couple in your congregation who can help.

When initially meeting with a pastor or counselor, you will need to tell the story of your husband's porn use and also convey your responses to his sin. Be clear and honest when sharing your perspective. In addition to this, completely answer any questions you are asked. Outsiders will be invited to enter your situation as you discuss information that focuses on the following questions:

1. Has your husband ever openly confessed specific sexual sins to you? Explain.

2. In this latest instance of sexual sin, did your husband confess his sin voluntarily or was the confession prompted by your questions? If it was prompted, what questions did you ask that drew out his confession? If he did not confess sin to you, what series of events has led you to believe that he is currently involved in sexual sin? (Example of a specific confession: Your husband said to you, "I watched pornography six times in the last two months and masturbated twice." Example of being caught: You discovered porn on his computer.)

3. Have his confessions of sexual sin up to this point been vague rather than specific? Has he been willing to fill in the gaps with additional details when asked? (Example of a vague confession: "Yes, I struggle sometimes.")

4. Has he willingly confessed his sexual sin to people other than you? If so, who and when?

5. Has he balked at prospective safeguards when you suggest them? (Possible safeguards include installing a router-based filter, finding accountability partners, adding accountability software, blocking tempting sites from his phone and other electronic devices, giving you passwords to all of his social media accounts and email accounts, allowing you to password protect his devices so that he cannot change the agreed-upon settings, etc.)

6. Has he welcomed the implementation of safeguards? Were those safeguards his idea or yours? Please share any accountability measures currently in place.

7. Does he sometimes confess sexual sin to you, but remain unwilling to tell others about his struggles? Has he asked you not to share his sin with others?

8. Does your husband know that you know about his porn use? If so, what was his response to you finding out? Was

it a sinful response? (Examples: He was angry and accused you of being a snoop. He shifted blame onto circumstances—"I was under a lot of stress"—or he blamed you—"If you'd be willing to have more sex, I wouldn't have these problems.") Or did he humbly confess his sin in brokenness? Explain.

9. Have you attempted to share with him ways that his sin hurts you and negatively impacts your family? If so, when? What did you share? How did he respond when you voiced concerns and sorrows?

10. Has he asked you to view porn with him or to participate in sexual acts that are scary, uncomfortable, or potentially harmful to your body?

11. Are the sexual encounters you have with your husband always consensual? Have you had any sexual encounters with your husband that were forced? If you aren't certain, here are some scenarios taken from *The Great Sex Rescue: The Lies You've Been Taught and How to Recover What God Intended* to help you diagnose whether you are experiencing sexual assault or lack of consent in your marriage:

- If your spouse is angry and potentially violent or verbally abusive, and you feel you have to have sex in order to protect yourself and your children.
- If your spouse routinely physically abuses you, and you find this happens less often if you have sex more.
- If your spouse routinely verbally abuses you and tells you that you are worthless or tells you that you will be disobeying God if you refuse sex.
- If your spouse doesn't give you access to money or groceries or toiletries unless you regularly have sex.
- If your spouse regularly has sex with you while you are sleeping (whether or not you wake up in the process), *unless you have explicitly stated beforehand that you actually want this.*

- If your spouse forces a sexual act that you do not want, that is also sexual assault, even if the rest of the sexual encounter was consensual.
- If your spouse threatens that if you do not have sex, he or she will look at porn, go on sex chat websites, go to strip clubs, or visit prostitutes.[1]

This will be a heavy conversation, but God will use it to shed light into the dark places in your marriage. There is hope for you in the difficulty because this initial discussion will give your counselor or pastor insights for moving forward. If your husband is repentant, at some point you will have a meeting with your counselor or pastor and your husband, where he will have an opportunity to confess his sin to them. But this initial meeting needs to occur without your husband present. In chapter 7 we will walk through the process of establishing accountability for your husband. Before that happens it's important that you secure the care and support you need. As I type these words I am praying for you that you will bravely let a few Christians into your life and that God will use the care they give to bring you comfort and healing. Bravery isn't the only thing you need right now; you also need wisdom. That's what we will consider next.

Questions for Action, Discussion, and Reflection

1. Where are you in the process of letting others into your struggle? What is the next step you need to take?

2. Can you recall ways that God has held you through the comforting embrace of accountability?

Further Reading on Accountability

Welch, Edward T. *Side By Side: Walking with Others in Wisdom and Love* (with study guide). Wheaton, IL: Crossway, 2015.

5

Wisdom from God

Before you begin this chapter, please read 1 Samuel 25.

DID YOU NOTICE anything unexpected about chapter 25 when you read it? Were you surprised that although this is a book about battling pornography, these verses don't mention sexual sin? Even so, this story is relevant to your marriage. Careful reflection on the lives of Nabal, David, and Abigail will reveal similarities between yourself, your husband, and the main characters and help you assess your responses to trials.

This is a tense point in history. King Saul is still ruling, but God has made it clear that in due time David will take over the throne because Saul rejected God's Word and defied his orders in battle. Because Saul is intent on tracking down and killing David, David and his army are continually in peril. They are fugitives on the move—hiding in the wilderness, in the mountains, and in caves. For a time, they inhabit the same area as Nabal's shepherds and flocks, where David's men keep them safe. Now the time has come to shear the sheep and celebrate the bounty of the season with a feast. David sends a message to Nabal requesting a portion of his abundance. This is reasonable given the protection they provided. Mary Evans notes, "Even without any service [David's army] might have rendered, normal rules of hospitality would have brought them some kind of positive response."[1] But Nabal declines in an incredibly rude way.

This introduction to Nabal sets the stage for the rest of the chapter. Even his name foreshadows the type of person he will prove to be. *Nabal* means a fool who doesn't understand what is right.[2] We also learn from a commentary about Nabal's lineage: "Calebites are an esteemed family of Judah, responsible for the founding of David's hometown, Bethlehem. Nabal was David's kinsman."[3] When David sends a message to Nabal, he refers to himself as "your son David" (v. 8). He is speaking rightly of their familial ties. He receives a scathing reply: "[Nabal] refuses to accept any connection with David. 'Your son David' of verse 8 is returned as Who is this son of Jesse? Nabal accepts Saul's assessment of David as a thankless rebel … (22:13–24:2), and he refuses to give any help."[4]

When Nabal adds insult to injury by calling the anointed king of his nation a runaway slave,[5] there is much at stake in this declaration. His assessment of David's status is not merely a vote cast for or against a political official. Rather, aligning with Saul over David is willful unbelief in God's promises. Nabal is not only selfish and foolish, he is also faithless. His reply to David has ignited the warrior's fury, and for the next several verses, devastation seems to be inevitable. But the story doesn't end in disaster because wisdom steps into the schism.

Abigail Demonstrated Wisdom

Abigail has become like a dear friend to me. I hope you feel the same way about her by the time you finish reading this book. God teaches David a crucial lesson through Abigail. Proverbs 11:30 says, "The fruit of the righteous is a tree of life, and the one who is wise saves lives" (NIV).[6] Which character in 1 Samuel 25 does this proverb remind you of? Abigail's heroic, lifesaving intervention happens along the road to David's ascension to the throne of Israel. This story is about a time when David learns to entrust God with his anger and desire for revenge. It's also about a discerning wife. Scripture describes her in two ways (1 Samuel 25:3). One of the phrases used means beautiful. The other is translated several ways—intelligent, sensible, discerning, of good understanding, and wise. No matter which version you are reading, it's safe to say that if Abigail was a member of your church today, she's the type of person you'd want to go to for advice.

What Is Wisdom?

In the next chapter we are going to look at some of the ways Abigail acted wisely in her relationships. But first, we'll look at the New Testament definition of wisdom. In the book of James, we are instructed to pursue wisdom. Here is what one commentator says about the wisdom James describes: "[Wisdom] is the moral discernment that enables the believer to meet life and its trials with decisions and actions consistent with God's will. Johnstone defines it as 'that queenly regulative discretion which sees and selects worthy ends, and the best means of attaining them.'"[7] Wouldn't you love to possess the ability to pick the best path and the most virtuous course of action when many options are available? I sure would. Here's something amazing—God wants you and I to have that ability too. This same wisdom that Abigail possessed is available to every single Christian, and James tells us how we can get it. He writes,

> If any of you lacks wisdom, let him ask God, who gives generously to all without reproach, and it will be given him. But let him ask in faith, with no doubting, for the one who doubts is like a wave of the sea that is driven and tossed by the wind. For that person must not suppose that he will receive anything from the Lord; he is a double-minded man, unstable in all his ways. (James 1:5–8)

This verse is the best sort of news! Are you unsure of what to do about all that has transpired in your marriage? God has exactly what you need. And it's free—all you have to do is ask him and trust that he will provide. John Newton says, "The chief means of attaining wisdom are the holy Scriptures and prayer. The one is the fountain of living water, the other the bucket with which we are to draw."[8] So while we are praying for God to grant his wisdom, let's also go to the Scriptures and see what he intends to give us. James was Jesus's brother. Few people had a better front-row seat for viewing wisdom in action than James. He gives us a definition of wisdom in his epistle. Jesus is the only person who has ever displayed wisdom perfectly, but as you consider Abigail's actions, you will see many ways that her dealings with her husband and David coincide with the comprehensive vision of wisdom that James lays out. He writes,

> Who is wise and understanding among you? By his good conduct let him show his works in the meekness of wisdom. But if you have bitter jealousy and selfish ambition in your hearts, do not boast and be false to the truth. This is not the wisdom that comes down from above, but is earthly, unspiritual, demonic. For where jealousy and selfish ambition exist, there will be disorder and every vile practice. But the wisdom from above is first pure, then peaceable, gentle, open to reason, full of mercy and good fruits, impartial and sincere. And a harvest of righteousness is sown in peace by those who make peace. (James 3:13–18)

True wisdom is "from above." Because it comes from God, it's only available to Christians. It encompasses every aspect of life. It's not just saying the right thing; it's also doing the right thing (v. 13). It starts with your motives (vv. 16, 17), which find expression through thoughts, words, and actions. It's so expansive that its potential for doing good fills the imagination and facilitates merciful, future-looking expressions of love.

Let's look more closely at the words James uses to describe true wisdom. As you read, I would like you to pray that God would give you specific wisdom to apply each facet to your marriage. Then start making a list of ways that each aspect of wisdom could help you relate more wisely to your husband. After reading chapter 6, revisit these principles again and look for the unique ways Abigail expresses them in her dealings with Nabal, her servants, David, and his army.

Wisdom Is Pure

First, wisdom is pure, and this purity is much more than just sexual purity. It has been described by others as both ceremonial purity and "sincere moral and spiritual integrity" and also "the submission of the entire personality to God."[9] Jesus describes in the beatitudes the kind of person who gets to see God. As one commentator writes, "The pure attain the vision of God which constitutes the highest wisdom" (Matthew 5:8).[10] This is one passage of Scripture I long to experience. It's also one that I pray frequently for people who are caught in sexual sin: "Father, please give them a pure heart so that they would be able to clearly see you in all the beauty of your holiness." This first description of wisdom as *pure* is the governing motivation for all of the following descriptors. *Pure* is also the word used to describe Jesus in 1 John 3:3.[11] Ask Jesus to help you identify and confess impurity in your life. Can you think of impure motivations, actions, thoughts, or words that you have directed toward your spouse? Confess those to Jesus and to your husband. Then ask God to cover them with his perfect purity.

Wisdom Is Peaceable

James is not calling for the kind of peace that requires you to sacrifice holiness. A truly peaceful person is also a righteous person, so there's no way to justify seeking peace if it means sacrificing moral integrity. A wise person willingly fights sin while at the same time "yearning to heal all divisions by wise counsel."[12] Are you the type of person who generally mends marital disputes or inflames them?[13] What about your other relationships— do you find yourself often at odds with family members, coworkers, or friends? What, if anything, in your life would need to change for you to become a peace-making person?

Wisdom Is Gentle

The word *gentle* "conveys respect for the feelings of others, being willing to waive all rigor and severity in one's dealings with others."[14] Acting in accordance with wisdom means that we won't treat those who have sinned against us with harshness (see Matthew 18:21–35), because we recognize that God has treated us with undeserved kindness.[15] Do you ever speak harshly to your husband and children? Would anyone who knows you think of you as exacting or severe? The next time you are frustrated with someone, stop and consider how you could speak to that person gently about whatever is frustrating you.

Wisdom Is Open to Reason

One New Testament scholar describes being open to reason as having "a temper that easily obeys."[16] Does this describe your attitude toward your spouse? Are you able to control your temper, even when he sins against you? Do you ever find yourself expressing anger toward him in uncontrolled ways? A person who is open to reason "is ready to cooperate when a better way is shown; it is the opposite of being stubborn and unyielding."[17] Be honest—would you want to have yourself as a teammate? How would those who know you best describe you? Are you cooperative or stubborn? Would they say that you're willing to consider a better course of action when it's brought to your attention? If you aren't sure, ask those who know you best for honest feedback.

Wisdom Is Full of Mercy and Good Fruits

Mercy sees people who are broken, hurting, or caught in sin and offers to help. Mercy doesn't treat people the way they deserve to be treated because it is marked by compassion.[18] If you are a Christian, God has treated you with mercy. He expects you to do the same for others. That's why James also tells us that "judgment is without mercy to one who has shown no mercy" (James 2:13). Would the people in your life say that your actions are marked by mercy and good fruits? Ask the person who is reading this book with you to help you honestly explore your current response to your husband for indications of mercy.

Wisdom Is Impartial

James had a lot to say about the sin of partiality (or favoritism) earlier in this epistle. Is this particular sin a struggle for you? Do you use people to get something you want from them? Do you ever treat people better (or worse) based on their social standing, wealth, level of education, or what you perceive they can do to elevate your status or make your life better? James says discrimination is the opposite of God's command to "love your neighbor as yourself" (James 2:1–10, Mark 12:31). Here are a few more definitions of the word impartial: "without variance (opposite of the duplicity of an uncontrolled tongue), unwavering, straight-forward, 'undivided in mind' does not cause division of disunity."[19] Are you the type of person who fosters unity or division in your relationships? It's such an important question that I'll pose it a second way: Do you enjoy bringing people together or driving wedges between them? Would those living and working with you describe you as straightforward or manipulative in your speech and actions toward them?

Wisdom Is Sincere

Sincerity strives to be genuine—not hypocritical—and consistent.[20] Try to recall some of the conversations you've had over the past week. Did you have moments when you were saying one thing and thinking something completely different? Do you feel like you must hide your attitudes and motives and pretend to be something you aren't? Do you act one way with certain friends and a different way with others? Does who you are on the inside match who you present to the world? Wise sincerity "does not need to work under a mask since it has nothing to hide."[21]

Wisdom Gives a Harvest of Righteousness

"And a harvest of righteousness is sown in peace by those who make peace" (James 3:18). This is my favorite part of the passage! The wisdom God gives makes our imaginations wise too. When you think about the future of your marriage, what do you envision? Do you have hopeful thoughts or hopeless ones? This verse tells us to expect and imagine that good fruit will grow out of our wise endeavors:

> The result of exercising heavenly wisdom is given in this concluding statement by James. He speaks of "fruit of righteousness" as being "sown." Although one commonly thinks of seed as being sown and fruit as being harvested, James is already thinking about the crop that will ultimately be harvested. He has the viewpoint of a farmer who understands in the broader sense that he is actually sowing a crop when he plants his seed.[22]

We can have such confidence in the effects of God's wisdom that even the seeds we sow can be referred to as fruit. Wise action is bursting with potential, and we can be confident when we act wisely that there's a harvest of righteousness ahead.

Wisdom Provides Strength

There's one more reason we need to petition God for wisdom when we face difficult trials. Douglas Moo reminds us that Jewish wisdom literature speaks of wisdom as essential for people who want to suffer well because it equips people to "endure trials with fortitude and godliness."[23] God's wisdom will strengthen you to plant fruit even as suffering persists. Next, we will look closely at the wisdom and courage of Abigail, who willingly confronted difficulties that arose because of her husband's sin. Let's see what we can learn from watching her work toward a peaceful resolution.

Questions for Action, Discussion, and Reflection

1. Reread 1 Samuel 25. In which verses do you see Abigail being (a) pure, (b) peaceable, (c) gentle, (d) open to reason, (e) full of mercy and good fruits, (f) impartial, (g) sincere, (h) sowing a harvest of righteousness in peace by making peace.

2. As you read through the characteristics of a wise person listed in question 1, which ones stand out as most evident in your life? Share an example.

3. As you read through the wisdom traits, did God bring to mind any deficits in your own life? Which areas of your life would benefit from growth in wisdom? Remember to pray and ask God to provide growth in these areas.

Further Reading on the Book of James

Hiebert, D. Edmond. *James*. Winona Lake, IN: BMH Books, 2002.

6

Abigail: A Wise Woman Who Did What She Could

Before you begin this chapter,
please reread 1 Samuel 25:14–35.

I DON'T KNOW the particulars of your story. Still, I can tell you with certainty that staying on the sidelines and remaining a passive observer of your spouse's sexual sin will result in further destruction. This chapter will help you focus on ways that God's grace has equipped you to wisely reclaim your marriage. Your husband, your struggling teammate, needs help. Abigail is the kind of helper I aim to be. She's an example for you to follow too. As you reflect on verses 14–20, questions about a wife's submission to her husband might arise for you. A full treatment of the topic of submission is beyond the scope of this book, but there are a few things that I would like you to remember while seeking to understand this text. First, Abigail was not a power-hungry wife seeking to rule over her husband. She wasn't vying for her husband's God-ordained leadership role. There is no indication that Abigail routinely went against her husband's decisions if she didn't agree with them. The humility we see in her encounter with David indicates that she was the type of wife who would have submitted to Nabal and gladly prepared provisions for David's men had Nabal asked her to do so, even if she didn't particularly feel like doing it. Second, she provides a beautiful example of how true submission responds when godly male leadership is absent in the home. Abigail was a wife demonstrating complete submission to God. She was a woman prepared to please her God no matter the cost.

Over the years, I have heard excellent sermons about how to submit to and respect my husband. What I haven't heard is a single sermon that teaches wives what to do when submitting to a sinful husband would mean rebelling against God. Wife, your submission to your husband has biblically defined limits. God doesn't want you to submit to your husband if doing so would mean committing or endorsing sin. Some Christians mistakenly depict ideal biblical femininity as passive and reserved. These descriptors don't describe the pinnacle of womanhood—they are neutral attributes that could be wise and appropriate responses in some situations and ill-advised and inappropriate in others. In cases such as Abigail's, when a foolish, selfish, self-indulgent husband acts in such a way that the consequences of his actions will bring harm upon his family, biblical femininity requires a godly wife to act. Abigail found it necessary to bypass her husband's sinful wishes in order to fully submit herself to God. Today we will look at the specific ways Abigail did this. As you consider her life, ask God to show you ways you can follow her example, and ask him to prepare you for decisive action.

Abigail Was Prepared for Decisive Action

The most important thing we will see is that Abigail trusted God's character. He was her motivation to advance toward difficulty. Abigail acted like a woman who believed God was with her. She demonstrated how to be a faithful wife even when her husband was so entrenched in sin that he partied hard while destruction loomed.

Your situation likewise necessitates action. Has it also brought to light perceived inadequacies and doubts that previously lurked quietly in the shadows of your mind? The confidence you will need to meet pain, loss, grief, and sin with boldness comes from continuing to remind yourself that you belong to God, who treasures you and is working relentlessly for your good. Because Abigail knew that God would deal justly with Nabal she didn't fight against him. Instead, she fought his sin and addressed its repercussions. Although he didn't see it, she was working for her husband. You are uniquely positioned to help your husband battle porn. Do not mistake your husband for an enemy. It's not your job to battle your husband—that's the mistake David made. Abigail saw the situation rightly. She placed her confidence in God's justice rather than in her ability to avenge wrong.

Can you imagine the intimidation Abigail must have felt as she descended into that "remote mountain ravine"[1] mere moments away from encountering David and several hundred additional armed warriors? One misstep could have cost Abigail her life. It would have been much easier to flee in the opposite direction, moving away from the conflict rather than toward it. When we compare her selfless confrontation to Nabal's apathetic self-centeredness, she shines as an example to follow. Abigail chose the most difficult route. She picked the course of action that had the greatest potential to bring about helpful change. It also involved the greatest personal risk. She chose to give sacrificial love, and her choice preserved her home.

Hindsight is 20/20, and we know that ultimately Abigail accomplished what she set out to do. However, the ending of your story hasn't yet unfolded. I think most women would act this boldly if they knew which actions would bring about effective change. The problem is that having your trust shattered has probably caused hope to dwindle (especially if you've lived many seasons with a husband who repeatedly pursues porn). Are you thinking, *My husband will never change? What good could I possibly accomplish? Why should I bother to take a stand for my marriage or for my difficult spouse when all of my hard work could easily be undone by another night of ogling?* Difficulty mounts when you consider that Scripture doesn't guarantee results. Your motivation to act can't come from what you hope will change in your unreliable husband. It must come from a settled trust in God's sovereignty.

I pray that your trust in God emboldens you to act in these ways: First, you can stand in the gap for your family by providing them any spiritual sustenance that they currently lack. Second, commit to pleasing God, even if this means going against your husband's desires. Third, you can intercede for your husband daily through prayer. Fourth, you can communicate relevant biblical truth. You can act courageously if you remain focused on God's character. You can't control the results, but you have a Savior who holds everything in his hands. He sees your worship. He sees your efforts to help your husband fight sin. He is pleased even if your best efforts don't seem to bring about the change you hope for.

When I think of steady resolve in the face of calamity, a scene from the movie *JoJo Rabbit* comes to mind. The movie depicts a family living in Nazi Germany during World War II. One day, as JoJo and his mother walked through the town square, they passed several citizens hanging dead—punished as criminals for resisting the Nazis. JoJo, who was a young boy, asked his mother what they had done to receive this punishment. She answered, "They did what they could."[2] That's the same resolve we see in Abigail— she did everything she could to help, even though the situation was very grim.

While discussing this moving scene from *JoJo Rabbit*, my friend Andrea Lee pointed me to Mark 14 because this same memorable phrase is found in the story of a woman who worshiped Jesus by anointing his head with expensive perfume. The people watching called her actions a waste. They rebuked her harshly because the perfume was worth more than a year's wages. They claimed the money would have been better spent on the poor (Mark 14:4–5). A few days later, this same woman saw her Savior crucified and placed in a tomb. I wonder if she second-guessed her bold, extravagant worship as she waited in the space between his death and resurrection?

As you wait, hoping God will breathe new life into your marriage, you might think your attempts to love your husband in the midst of his sin have been a waste. Jesus doesn't share your doubts. If your resolve to serve your home is motivated by love for Jesus, then it is worship. Jesus said of the woman who anointed him, "She has done a beautiful thing to me . . . *she has done what she could*; she has anointed my body beforehand for burial" (Mark 14:6, 8; emphasis added). Jesus affirms the value of your devoted actions (Hebrews 10:6). He accepts your worship and calls it a beautiful gift.

It is not your job to accept responsibility for your husband's sins; they are his to own. But as you imagine Abigail prostrate before King David, willing to incur blame for her husband's offenses even though those sins were not hers, let your mind be drawn to the work of your Savior. He suffered for all your sins and bore all your transgressions. As he bled and died and lay for three days in the tomb, his work on the cross looked like a waste. But it wasn't—resurrection was coming. When he rose out of that tomb, he freed you and me from sin. His Spirit will provide the resolve to continue serving others selflessly. When he calls you to action, you can trust him with the results. He is more than capable of accomplishing all the good he intends in and through your life. Sometimes the loving acts that end in apparent defeat are sowing seeds of new life. These will burst forth in due time.

Abigail Made an Impact

How big an impact can a solitary wife make as she takes a bold stand against her husband's sin? How much suffering might come from the ripples I produce? These types of questions might have run through Abigail's mind as she raced to pack enough provisions to feed 600 warriors. What was she thinking and feeling as she bowed facedown in the dirt before 400 battle-hardened soldiers? What shape did her urgent prayers to God take as she asked him to use her peace offering to placate an army intent on slaughtering her household? I look forward to asking her when we meet in heaven. If you are weighing whether or not your husband and marriage are worth whatever bold and selfless actions God may call you to perform in the uncertain days to come, the answer is a resounding yes! If your actions are motivated by love for your Savior, all the good you do for your husband will be received by Jesus as beautiful worship. Love is risky. Love requires action. Love means being willing to fight the sin that is infecting your husband's soul. Love never fails.

Keep all this in mind as we look to see what we can learn from Abigail's discerning course of action in the following perilous situation:

> But one of the young men told Abigail, Nabal's wife, "Behold, David sent messengers out of the wilderness to greet our master, and he railed at them. Yet the men were very good to us, and we suffered no harm, and we did not miss anything when we were in the fields, as long as we went with them. They were a wall to us both by night and by day, all the while we were with them keeping the sheep. Now therefore know this and consider what you should do, for harm is determined against our master and against all his house, and he is such a worthless man that one cannot speak to him."
>
> Then Abigail made haste and took two hundred loaves and two skins of wine and five sheep already prepared and five seahs of parched grain and a hundred clusters of raisins and two hundred cakes of figs, and laid them on donkeys. And she said to her young men, "Go on before me; behold, I come after you." But she did not tell her husband Nabal. And as she rode on the donkey and came down under cover of the mountain, behold,

David and his men came down toward her, and she met them. (1 Samuel 25:14–20)

Abigail employed her agency to protect the well-being of her household by boldly opposing Nabal's sinful desires. I define "agency" as the ability to use the rich wisdom found in the Bible, along with your heart, your mind, and your bodily strength, to continue serving God and loving your neighbor, regardless of how bleak the situation may seem.

Living through a pandemic provided me with a fresh perspective regarding the imminent peril Abigail faced. The events of 2020 and 2021 changed the way I think about Abigail's encounter with David. We watched helplessly as COVID-19 advanced across the globe and claimed millions of lives. We heard stories from friends around the world—some couldn't leave their small apartments for weeks on end. Others spoke of overburdened hospitals unable to provide emergency care, which left people to nurse gravely ill family members at home. In some places, dead bodies of loved ones were placed on the curbs outside of homes (where they would sometimes sit for a few days) waiting for collection trucks to retrieve them for burial.

This devastating virus gave me insights into how scared Abigail must have felt as she faced David. His forces were bigger and stronger than she was, and they were poised to attack her loved ones. Abigail was vulnerable. That's how I felt when the pandemic struck. It revealed my weakness. At the same time, it clarified my responsibilities. We must hold these two realities in tension. Even as I sprang into action buying toilet paper, masks, and other necessities to care for my family, it was clear that my success in caring for my household was (and still is) utterly dependent on God at every point. That reminder gave me great comfort. It was my job to go to the store and buy the supplies we needed. It was my job to wash my hands when I arrived home. It was my job to practice social distancing for a season. I used my agency to meet these reasonable expectations. I served God by being responsible. As I did these things, I asked my Heavenly Father to do what I could not do—preserve my family and end a pandemic. Any success that ever comes from my work (or yours) has been passed to us from God's abundant storehouse of provision.

Like Abigail, your husband's sin has left you vulnerable. Keep calling out to the Lord for strength and help. He is mighty and able to rescue.

Has awareness of newly discovered porn or the ongoing threat of recurring porn ever filled you with dread? Porn is a lurking enemy. It has infected your husband and thereby threatens the well-being of your marriage. God has called your husband to lead and protect his family. If he refuses to stand up and fight his sin, you will have to take a stand. Truly standing for your family means being willing to take a stand against your husband's sin.

When crisis strikes her home, Abigail models a beautiful facet of biblical femininity—the willingness to stand in the gap for her family. As with the pandemic, there are many aspects of your current suffering that are completely outside your control (including your husband's decision to continue this behavior or change), but this does not mean you are powerless. Do not be tricked into believing that the success of your actions depends on your husband's repentance. There's no indication that Nabal repented, yet Abigail successfully brought about good for her family. For the Christian, success is measured in terms of faithfulness to God and his word. God chose to give you agency! This is not the time to shrivel up; don't let disengagement from daily life in your household become the new norm. This is the time to stand firm and press on. You have God's Spirit to strengthen you in weakness. His power at work within you is the same power that raised Jesus from the dead (Romans 8:11)!

Maybe today your husband hasn't even started down the path of trusting Jesus and submitting himself to God's word. Maybe he is a stumbling, irresolute man who speaks of desiring freedom from sexual sin but is inconsistent in his actions. Maybe he is working to slowly regain your trust by exhibiting increasingly consistent growth after many years marked by persistent porn use. Whatever the case may be, Abigail's valiant, decisive service to her family leads every wife to wonder, *What can I do, after considering how my husband is currently leading (or choosing not to lead) my family, to promote the physical, emotional, and spiritual well-being of my household? What actions can I take to help my family flourish (either to complement my husband's Godward leadership or to shield my family from the negative effects of my husband's ungodly leadership)?* Let's look in more depth at each of the specific ways every woman whose husband struggles with porn can stand in the gap for her family—committing to providing spiritual food, resolving to please God regardless of the cost, interceding for your husband and communicating truth. As you read them, prayerfully consider ways to implement these things (if you aren't already doing them). God might supply additional ideas for uniquely serving your household. Write them down as they come to mind.

Commit to Providing Spiritual Food

First, commit to providing spiritual sustenance for your family. In the same way that you and your family require necessities like shelter, food, and water, your family also needs spiritual provisions. If your husband is not providing them right now, it is your job to do so. There are four spiritual provisions every family needs: the church, regular Bible reading, Scripture memory, and prayer. Below are several investigative questions to help you determine that these basic spiritual needs are being met:

1. Are you currently a member of a church that faithfully teaches the Bible? Do you attend worship services regularly? If not, finding a church home and prioritizing attendance is of first importance. This is the shelter your family

needs right now. The church will help you weather the storm that is raging in your marriage.

2. Do you read the Bible regularly? If not, start with one chapter each day. Later in this book we will spend time in the gospel of Luke. That's a great place to start. Read it from the beginning. Snuggle up on the couch and read it out loud to your children. Another great option is a Bible reading app. My church is reading through several books of the Bible this year—one chapter each day. During dinner my family listens to a chapter. Afterwards, we discuss it. Curtis and I ask our sons simple questions. We ask, what happened in that chapter? What was the main point? What does this chapter teach us about God? Do you have any questions about what we listened to/read today?

3. After you read the Bible, pray (as a family, if possible). Have each person pray for the following three things:

   - Thank God for something you enjoyed today. (His blessings are abundant!)

   - Ask God for his forgiveness for a sin or for help with one thing that concerns you today. (This is a great time to model humble confession. Were you rude or short tempered toward your kids today? Admit that and ask them for forgiveness. Tell them that you are a sinner who needs Jesus too! When you pray out loud, remember to also ask God for forgiveness.)

   - Think of one person you know who is suffering, sick, or sad and ask God to help them.

4. Do you memorize Scripture? Start with verses that remind you of God's care for you. Deuteronomy 31:6 says God will never leave you. Psalm 127:1 recounts that God is the one who brings success to our endeavors. Concentrate on one verse at a time. If you have children, have them memorize with you and talk to them about God's character. We give our kids one verse at a time to memorize, and we review it

with them several times each week. When they were little, we rewarded them with a small prize from the (incredibly tacky yet endearing) treasure chest that my husband built with the boys and then spray-painted gold.

You can provide spiritual sustenance to your family. Do not delay. These things are simple, and most of them take only a few minutes each day, but they are the difference between starvation and growth.

Resolve to Please God Regardless of the Cost

The second way you can stand in the gap for your family is by resolving to please God even if doing so displeases your husband. Consider my suggestions, but before implementing this step, please dialogue with your counselor and come up with a wise course of action together. If your husband has not yet voluntarily shared his struggle with another Christian man who would encourage him to implement effective accountability, then this step may start with resolving to share your husband's porn use with one other Christian man who would be willing to help him. If no one comes to mind, ask your pastor or counselor to help you identify a person who fits this description. We talked about the significance of honesty in chapter 3, and this is a crucial way to put truth telling into practice. Your husband might not prefer this course of action. Having sin exposed is embarrassing and uncomfortable. Abigail did not consult Nabal before she took provisions to David's men. She already knew her actions were in direct opposition to Nabal's desires. She understood that pleasing God would require her to go against her husband's desires.

Because I don't know you personally I can't speak directly to your marriage, but below are a few suggestions in addition to getting accountability for your husband that could be wise responses. If they seem relevant, please discuss them with your counselor before applying them. These are measures to protect your family by making porn less accessible in your home. These are especially pertinent if your children have been exposed to porn because of your husband's online activity. Making your home as safe as possible is one way to love your household. Even if you don't have children at home, working to keep porn at bay is a way of caring for your spouse. It's impossible to cut off all access to porn, but there are some ways to lessen the onslaught:

1. Does your home computer have accountability software? Is the computer in a public space with the screen facing outward? What, if anything, would stop you from implementing these safeguards?
2. Are there streaming services that have been a source of temptation that you could cancel? Does your internet have a router-based filter that's set to block adult content? If not, would you consider contributing to the well-being of your household by installing one?
3. Has porn been accessed through gaming consoles or other unnecessary devices? Would you be willing to serve your family by removing them from your home?

If you are hesitant to take this step, discuss your reasons with your counselor. This moment might be a crossroad in your marriage. If so, it's time for you to decide if you will be a merciful friend to your husband (if you currently consider him an enemy, remember that Jesus tells us in Matthew 5:44 to love our enemies). Apart from Christ, hating our enemies is a natural response, but Christians shouldn't rejoice when their enemies are defeated by sin. Resolve to love your husband like a friend. For our friends, we desire victory. Left unchecked, sexual sin will triumph over your husband. Do you want to see him defeated? By keeping his sin secret, you are treating him as an enemy—leaving him alone in the dark to be devoured by his own sinful passions. God is calling you to show your husband love, and this will require you to respond to his sin bravely and boldly. He might not be strong enough to fight porn right now. God has sovereignly placed you at a vantage point where you can see his dilemma more clearly than others can. Praise God that he has given you spiritual eyes to see the devastation looming just beyond the horizon. Praise God that he has uncovered your husband's transgressions to you and given you agency to act! Your bold opposition to pornography might be one of the best gifts God ever gives your husband. We will discuss the specifics of accountability after porn thoroughly in the next chapter, but these practical steps must be preceded by the realization that ongoing, loving accountability is the best path toward lasting change.

Intercede for Your Husband

Enduring change comes from the same God who tells us that in Christ we can approach his throne confidently (Hebrews 4:16). Abigail's intervention required her to humbly intercede before David. It's not likely that you will end up kneeling before the ruler of your country and asking him to give your spouse another chance. But this critical moment is an opportunity to kneel before your heavenly father and ask him to work in and for your husband in mighty and specific ways. Consistent prayer on behalf of another is a powerful way to love and serve that person, while also standing up to sin. In Matthew 5:44 Jesus not only tells us to love our enemies, he also says to pray for people who persecute us. Learning to intercede on behalf of a spouse who chooses to sin against us, is another way we can become more like Christ. Keep your list of prayer prompts on hand, and continue to pray daily for your husband. Persist in this practice even if repentance doesn't come soon. Abigail truly was a woman who intervened in every way she could. Can the same be said of you?

Let's envision once again Abigail's still frame, bowing quietly in the dirt as the chaos of seething anger and ruthless vengeance

rush toward her. Remember that the full force of her ample, courageous confidence in God brought her to this frightening moment.
As she faithfully confronts David, she imparts to us courage for
our own marriages.

> When Abigail saw David, she hurried and got down
> from the donkey and fell before David on her face and
> bowed to the ground. She fell at his feet and said, "On me
> alone, my lord, be the guilt. Please let your servant speak
> in your ears, and hear the words of your servant. Let not
> my lord regard this worthless fellow, Nabal, for as his
> name is, so is he. Nabal is his name, and folly is with him.
> But I your servant did not see the young men of my lord,
> whom you sent. Now then, my lord, as the LORD lives,
> and as your soul lives, because the LORD has restrained
> you from bloodguilt and from saving with your own
> hand, now then let your enemies and those who seek to
> do evil to my lord be as Nabal. And now let this present
> that your servant has brought to my lord be given to the
> young men who follow my lord. Please forgive the tres-
> pass of your servant." (1 Samuel 25:23–28a)

Abigail's speech, which begins in verse 24 and continues
through verse 31, is the longest given by a woman in the Old Testament—153 Hebrew words.[3] This entreaty reveals an important
contrast between Abigail's encounter with her servant (vv. 14–22)
and her address to David. These two interactions clarify certain
distinctions between gossip and loving, constructive conversation. The servant asked Abigail to act because "(Nabal) is such a
worthless man that one cannot speak to him" (v. 17). Abigail listened and took his request seriously, but we do not see her venting about her husband's bad behavior. It is not until Abigail spoke
to David, the only person who had the power to call off the attack
on her family, that she openly declared her husband's sin. Abigail

modeled self-control by passing up an opportunity to gossip with her servant and by reserving her words for a moment when they were likely to bring the most benefit to Nabal.

Abigail decisively entered the conflict between David and her husband, yet her boldness was accompanied by humility (vv. 23, 24). Keep this same humility front and center. You are not responsible for producing ideal outcomes, because you can't produce them. You can humbly submit results to God, even if your attempts at reconciliation and service result in no apparent changes in your husband's behavior.

In this passage we also see that Abigail spoke honestly about the situation. She was willing to call foolishness, foolishness (v. 25). Her words here are neither gossip nor disrespect. She was giving a truthful assessment of the situation while working to bring about a peaceful resolution to the problem Nabal created. In Proverbs 5:22–23, a father warns his son about the dangers of adultery: "The iniquities of the wicked ensnare him, and he is held fast in the cords of his sin. He dies for lack of discipline, and because of his great folly he is led astray." Folly is another word for foolishness. Scripture is clear that sexual sin is foolish. The only biblically faithful option is to define your husband's sin the same way God does.

Communicate Truth

Another way we can imitate Abigail is by recalling and communicating truths about God in accordance with Scripture. This can be clearly seen in the end of her speech to David:

> For the LORD will certainly make my lord a sure house, because my lord is fighting the battles of the LORD, and evil shall not be found in you so long as you live. If men rise up to pursue you and to seek your life, the life of my lord shall be bound in the bundle of the living in the care

of the LORD your God. And the lives of your enemies he shall sling out as from the hollow of a sling. And when the LORD has done to my lord according to all the good that he has spoken concerning you and has appointed you prince over Israel, my lord shall have no cause of grief or pangs of conscience for having shed blood without cause or for my lord taking vengeance himself. And when the LORD has dealt well with my lord, then remember your servant. (1 Samuel 25:28b–31)

To follow Abigail's lead, we need to be diligent students of the Bible. There are many benefits that come from regularly studying Scripture. Reading the Bible is the best way to get to know God better. Communion with God, who loves you perfectly, will act as a healing balm during a time when communion with your husband has been fractured by his sin. Familiarizing yourself with Scripture is also the best way to prepare yourself to face trials faithfully. Abigail was well-acquainted with biblical truth. Did you notice the imagery she used in verse 29? Her example to David was timely and appropriate. It may have also comforted her as she kneeled before his vast army. She recalled aloud David's battle with Goliath—a young boy armed with a slingshot defeating a giant with a sword. This incredibly wise woman reminded David of the truth that was most pertinent to his situation: God would be faithful to fight David's battles.

The book of James ends with this thought about wayward sinners: "My brothers, if anyone among you wanders from the truth and someone brings him back, let him know that whoever brings back a sinner from his wandering will save his soul from death and will cover a multitude of sins." (James 5:19–20) This rescuer of the wayward sounds a lot like Abigail. This also sounds like the kind of wife your husband needs right now—one who is determined to help a sinner come back to the truth.

Questions for Action, Discussion, and Reflection

1. Is your family currently attending church, reading the Bible, memorizing Scripture, and praying together? If not, discuss with a friend your plan for beginning these life-sustaining practices. Make a list of local churches you intend to visit. Set aside specific times of day for Bible reading, verse memorization, and family prayer. Pick a book of the Bible to read. Decide on the first verse you will memorize.

2. Are there other ways you are currently standing in the gap for your family? If so, discuss them with your friend or journal about them.

3. In this chapter, we looked at specific ways Abigail serves as an example for women whose husbands are foolish and self-indulgent. Name them. Which one do you find most helpful? In what ways is it helpful?

Further Reading on Spiritual Disciplines

Mathis, David. *Habits of Grace: Enjoying Jesus through the Spiritual Disciplines*. Wheaton, IL: Crossway, 2016.

Whitney, Donald S. *Spiritual Disciplines for the Christian Life*. Colorado Springs, CO: NavPress, 2014.

7

Held by Jesus: Establishing Effective Accountability

SOMETIMES LOVE COMES in the form of comfort and encouragement. Those were the first things I received from the church as a young convert. As I matured in my faith, I learned that offering comfort is just one of many ways the members of a church care for one another. There are times God also calls the church to lovingly correct and rebuke wayward members. One word that encompasses many of the ways church members support each other is *accountability*. By this, I mean a willingness to give and receive care, spiritual support, oversight, and companionship within a faith community. People were not created to experience life alone. In order to stay on course and continue growing in Christlikeness, we all need the input of a church community. During this difficult time in your marriage, the accountability of a local church is God's gift to you.

I hope by now you have taken steps toward letting a local congregation into your situation so that they can understand how to best serve and love your family. This fellowship isn't just for your benefit. Your husband also needs the care of the church. There are four things I would like you to consider as you (hopefully in collaboration with your husband) think about establishing effective accountability for your spouse, specifically as it applies to battling pornography:

1. the importance of accountability, specifically within your local church;
2. seeking continuity in accountability;
3. your unique role as a wife in your husband's accountability process; and
4. steps toward growing effective accountability.

Today the song "Hold Me Jesus" is even more meaningful to me than it was in high school. That's because now I understand it in its context. In recent years I attended a lecture about Rich Mullins given by Andrew Peterson, and he shared the story behind the lyrics. Mullins's love for God and Scripture shines brightly through his music, but like the rest of us, he was a struggling sinner marked by contradictory behaviors. One of Mullins's tours took him to Amsterdam. While he was there, he decided he would visit a prostitute in the red-light district. There was only one major obstacle to this plan. He was sharing a hotel room with his manager. Since his manager always snored, Mullins decided to stay awake until he heard snoring. Once he was confident that his manager was sound asleep, he would slip out of the room undetected. When the appointed night arrived, the plan unraveled. His manager never snored that night. So Rich was sleepless in his bed, wrestling with God.[1] Out of that lust-filled night, an adult's lullaby was born.

As a teen, I sang the second verse over my own fears and anxiety, and I imagined God's gentle embrace, but Peterson clarified the meaning. This song isn't about asking God for a hug. It's about pleading with Jesus to restrain us. What Rich Mullins acknowledged about that fraught night in Amsterdam was that he needed Jesus to hold him back from things that could ruin him. The imagery here is akin to a master holding firmly to a leash while his tethered dog strains against him.[2]

The Importance of Accountability

Can you recall a time when you needed to be restrained from a sinful desire? How did God hold you back? In this example, God's help came in the form of accountability. Mullins's absence might have been noticed. He stayed in bed because he was unwilling to risk his reputation (and his job). During that restless interlude, God worked in him to bring him to repentance. We can see this process reflected in lyrics that recall contending with God before eventually submitting to his will. Rich's manager's presence didn't change his desires that night because accountability can't ever change a person's heart. What it can do is create distance between a person and his or her temptations. Many times that distance provides a space in which the Spirit moves to bring about conviction and change. God uses varying means to sanctify his children, but when it comes to fighting sexual temptation, accountability is a fundamental tool God uses to hold his children back from sin.

In one sense, the necessity of accountability for struggling Christians is more imperative today than it was for Rich Mullins in Amsterdam. The immediacy of technology has altered the landscape. We no longer have to sneak outside for a back-alley rendezvous. Much of the sexual sin committed by church members today takes place alone, at home behind closed doors. Pornography lures many by offering the guise of anonymity. I have never heard of a Christian hosting a porn-viewing party. This is a secretive sin. Therefore, many Christians assume that the best way forward is to confess this sin privately to God. Furthermore, embarrassment often prevents struggling believers from getting support and help. Access to prostitutes has certainly changed with time, but accountability after sexual sin is no less relational today than when the repentant prostitute anointed Jesus's feet.

Let's take a look at the Gospel of Luke and see how Jesus bestowed accountability on the former prostitute who crashed a dinner party to worship him. The passage begins with this description: "And behold, a woman of the city, who was a sinner" (Luke 7:37a). It's clear that Jesus's interaction with this woman wasn't a showcase in his traveling road show. She wasn't an anonymous display of the great things he had done in remote regions. This woman hadn't trailed Jesus until she journeyed a safe distance away from folks who knew her in order to secretly shower affections on her Savior. The people dining at Simon's house shunned her because she was locally recognized for her sinful lifestyle. Kenneth Bailey notes several important things about this situation:

> The story leaves us no doubt regarding the authenticity of her repentance. Yet we are also told that she is a resident of that same city and it is clear that she is known to Simon. If Simon and his other religious friends do not accept the authenticity of her repentance, no restoration to the community will take place. The Lost Sheep is brought back to the fold. The Prodigal Son is returned to the family. Zacchaeus is "also a son of Abraham" and can no longer be rejected as an outsider according to Jesus (Luke 19:9). So here, Simon must be led to see the authenticity of her repentance so that she will be restored to fellowship in her community.[3]

Not only does Jesus set right the audience's incorrect evaluation of her spiritual standing, he also gives her a grace-empowered opportunity to live out the repentance she claims. As she went forth from Simon's house to walk in newness of life, she had the added safety net of watchful neighbors.

Porn uncouples sexual sin from sexual intimacy—stripping it of both relationship and covenant exclusivity. Pornography lacks human connection but is still an invasive form of sexual expression. Anonymity has been lent to a category of relational sin that in the past the church was required to deal with publicly. Jesus chose to restore the repentant prostitute publicly. The church must ask itself what form of reconciliation will be most loving to the repentant porn user? Surely it will be much harder to avoid the temptations of sexual sin when confession remains solely between God and the sinner. Repentant sexual sinners still need the watching eyes and helping hands of a community.

In a sinless world, there would be no sexual expression apart from marital union. Pornography twists the fabric of God's created order by attempting to create an untenable oxymoron—anonymous relational sin. Pornography perverts God's plan by presenting sex as detached, impersonal, and unrestricted. Pornography does not deliver on these promises. The shame and guilt that comes from uncoupling sexual expression from marriage makes sinners want to hide, but concealing sin compounds the problem because reconciliation can't happen unless your spouse confesses his sexual sin to both God and you.

Seeking Continuity

Scripture exhorts Christians to bring sin out of isolation by confessing it to one another (James 5:16). Sexual sin is difficult to talk about, so you or your husband might try to avoid the awkwardness of face-to-face confession by seeking accountability from a long-distance friend. If you are not yet established in a local church, this option might be helpful temporarily, but emails, texting, and video chats cannot replace the church and its weekly in-person fellowship. In some cases, the best care might come from a long-distance friend, but even then, your husband will need additional support from a few local friends who spend time with him regularly and are kept updated on his struggle.

Another common pitfall is one-off confessions. Has your spouse jumped from person-to-person, never confessing to the same individual more than a few times? It's important to pick friends who will be part of your life for the foreseeable future. Continuity in accountability will help the person providing your husband care to recognize long-term patterns in his sin struggles. The ones offering care need to know the whole backstory and be kept updated if new problems arise in the future.

If you don't already have regular in-person interactions with other Christians who know about your marital difficulties, then prayerfully seek out this type of relationship. If no one comes to mind, ask your pastor if there's an older, wiser couple who might consider supporting you and your husband through an accountability relationship. Your local church is the best place to get accountability to help your spouse fight sexual temptation and to help you walk in forgiveness. God brings healing through accountability in the local church.

It is important to note that accountability is profitable for others, as well as the one seeking to break free from the snare of sin. Simon and his dinner guests were made privy to Jesus's interaction with this woman for their spiritual good as well as hers. Much good comes from watching God change a known sinner. Accountability allows those involved to see the restoration process firsthand. Think about the mutual benefits of revealed grace at Simon's house: The woman received a safety net. The people in attendance knew her history and her commitment to forsake sin. The hypocritical religious naysayers saw her genuine love for God and her humble worship, which served as a rebuke and a beacon inviting them to experience true faith. Granted, this was a difficult and awkward exchange. Accountability is rarely comfortable, but it is a necessary mode of edification for every reformed sinner. If the church is going to beat its porn habit, the people of God will have to embrace accountability.

A Spouse's Role in Accountability

There are certainly pitfalls to be avoided when offering accountability to your spouse. If you have previously made the mistake of inappropriate surveillance (as discussed in chapter 3), you might have withdrawn yourself from his accountability network. I hope after reading this you will reengage. As a wife, you have an indispensable, God-given role in the process. As you think about your duty, remember that all sin (including sexual sin) is first and foremost an offense against God. As 1 Corinthians 6:13b–15 says:

> The body is not meant for sexual immorality, but for the Lord, and the Lord for the body. And God raised the Lord and will also raise us up by his power. Do you not know that your bodies are members of Christ? Shall I then take the members of Christ and make them members of a prostitute? Never!

These verses were written in the context of a culture that esteemed men as more valuable than women. Women did not have equal rights within marriage. However, God doesn't pander to cultural biases. This is evident in the way that Paul demolishes prejudice by affirming the status of wives: "For the wife does not have authority over her own body, but the husband does. *Likewise the husband does not have authority over his own body, but the wife does*" (1 Corinthians 7:4; emphasis added). Let these passages motivate you towards holy jealousy. There is much at stake when your husband interacts with digital prostitutes! Scripture makes it clear that his body belongs to you. Therefore, you have the responsibility to call him to repentance and bring in help even before he repents (Galatians 6:1)!

It's also important to note that if your husband is using 1 Corinthians 7:4 to pressure you to engage in sexual acts that are unhealthy, frightening, painful, or unsafe, then he is misusing Scripture to justify heinous sin. While husbands and wives have mutual authority over each other's bodies, this authority has limits, just as a wife's biblical submission to her own husband has limits. Husbands and wives may not treat each other's bodies in ways that violate God's tender design for sexual intimacy. Sexual abuse and porn use often go hand in hand because the porn industry continues to find new ways to debase individuals and warp the joys of sexual intimacy. As I write this, viewing violent porn is becoming mainstream.[4] As a result, it is more common for women to be asked by their sexual partners to engage in sexual acts that are frightening, painful, and harmful. It would be naive to assume that such scenarios will not impact women within the church. So please know that it is abusive for your husband to ask you participate in sexual acts that scare you, intentionally cause pain, or threaten your safety. If this has ever happened to you, please read appendix 1, "Porn and Abuse," before taking any of the steps outlined in this chapter.

Paul says that your body belongs to your husband. He also says that husbands are to treat their wives the way Jesus treats the church. Jesus always approaches his bride (the church) with gentleness. He always loves and protects his people. Jesus stands in harm's way for his beloved—even to the point of laying down his life. Your husband is called to these high standards of caring for you and your body. Lengthier discussion of God's design for sex is beyond the scope of this book, but if you skipped ahead to this section, chapter 4 also provided further examples of sexual abuse that should help you discern, with the help of your counselor or pastor, whether or not your husband has been misusing his authority in this area.

We have talked about the definition of accountability, the necessity of accountability within every local church, seeking continuity in accountability, and a wife's right to play a central role in the accountability process. Now we will discuss some practical steps to take, along with necessary questions to ask, as you employ targeted accountability that is meant to help reduce specific temptations. Do not bypass these steps. They are a crucial way of showing your husband love.

Steps to Accountability

There are many questions that you should ask your husband, but there are some that aren't helpful. Questions that seek to merely satisfy your curiosity will not aid the reconciliation process. For example, it would not be wise to encourage him to recap specific scenes or images from the porn he has viewed. Misplaced jealousy might leave you wondering what kind of women he finds attractive. This unhelpful curiosity fails to remember that any of his sexual cravings for women other than you are misdirected. Obtaining information about the appearances of specific digitally enhanced seductresses is counterproductive. Recapping specifics could rekindle his lust and fuel your despair or rage.

The following list of questions is not exhaustive. It is meant to get the conversation started. The information shared will be extremely difficult to hear. It is appropriate to grieve and lament all that is disclosed. The sins your husband has committed have wounded you deeply, but the goal of these questions is not to inflict more wounds. They are intended to provide information that can help you fight future sin together in a targeted way. They are meant, much like a painful surgery and subsequent rehabilitation period, to address an existing injury in a way that facilitates healing. Asking poignant questions draws out truth and gives a clear picture of what temptations are most enticing. These trigger points will benefit from additional safeguards. The questions that follow are to be answered by your husband in the presence of you and your counselor and/or pastor. They will help everyone present at the meeting gain a clearer picture of the scope of his sin.

1. Where do you go to find pornographic media (i.e., specific websites, social media outlets, streaming services, etc.)?
2. Have you spent any money on sexual experiences? If so, when, how, and how much?

3. Has the sin of porn use been accompanied by other forms of sexual sin (e.g., visiting strip clubs or prostitutes, masturbating, sexting, live chatting, or interacting sexually with women or men online or in-person)?

4. What other sins has your porn use fostered (e.g., lying, abusing alcohol or drugs to numb the guilt, etc.)?

5. Do other forms of excessive indulgence often precede or follow your porn use (e.g., overspending, overeating, drunkenness, etc.)?

6. Have you ever viewed homosexual, child, or violent porn? If so, explain. (If someone discloses active use or possession of child pornography, this is a crime that falls under mandatory reporting statutes in most jurisdictions and needs to be reported to the authorities.)

7. What scenarios provide the greatest temptation toward sexual sin (e.g., at work on the night shift, alone at home for the weekend while spouse travels, hotel rooms on overnight business trips, downtime after a stressful day at work, etc.)?

8. What was the age of onset for your first experience with pornography and any other premarital sexual experiences you've had (including any sexual abuse you may have experienced)?

9. When and where are you viewing porn?

10. How many times a day/week/month/year are you viewing porn?

11. How often do you masturbate?

12. How long do you view porn per session?

13. What specific lies have you told to hide your porn use?

14. Have you found or utilized any loopholes within the safeguards that are currently used to keep your electronic devices free of porn? If so explain.

15. Has any sin come to mind that I am not asking you about that you have yet to confess?

Once you have a better understanding of your husband's particular sin, you can work with your counselors to develop an ongoing accountability plan for the days, weeks, months, and years to come. Here are a few more details to consider as you care for him in targeted ways:

- Talk with your spouse about setting aside an agreed-upon time for him to give you an update on how he is doing in regard to fighting sexual temptation. You will have the freedom to ask about his growth and struggles at other times, but schedule a regular check-in (that he is responsible for maintaining) to alleviate the difficulty of wondering *When is the right time to ask these hard questions?* This regular update could happen weekly or perhaps monthly, depending on his current level of struggle.
- Is your husband a believer, and is he repentant? If the answer to both is yes, then he has probably already voluntarily confessed his sin to a wise, local Christian friend, but if he hasn't, encourage him to do so without delay. Ask your husband to commit to regular check-ins with his brother in Christ. Additionally, your husband will benefit from the oversight of a pastor, elder, Sunday school teacher, or community group leader within your local church. This person should be in a position of spiritual authority over your husband and be committed to encouraging him in his faith, praying for him, and asking for regular updates on how he is dealing with sexual temptations, as well as inquiring about the well-being of your family, marriage, and your spouse's overall spiritual health.
- Does your husband say he is a Christian while continuing unrepentant in his sin? For this situation, you also need to seek counsel from one of your pastors or elders to apply Matthew 18. This passage gives the church a process called church discipline to confront people who are unrepentant

and encourage them to forsake sin. If your church does not practice church discipline, it would be wise to consider finding a church in your area that does because this loving process is one of the means God uses to bring hardened sinners to repentance. Pursuing an unrepentant husband through church discipline is a fundamental way to show him care.

- Is your husband an unbeliever? If so (and assuming you are a Christian), God has given you an enduring community—the local church. Remember how my church family loved and supported me during my parents' divorce? It has long been my prayer that every person could experience the outpouring of love that I have received from the church during my lifetime! Your church will be able to walk with you through the complexities of having a spouse who doesn't share your sexual ethic.

In addition to working alongside your husband to establish an ongoing accountability plan, another important part of the reconciliation process is taking time to communicate with your husband ways that his sins have affected you and your children. If your husband is repentant, this could happen at some point after he confesses his sin to you. If your husband is unrepentant, it would be wisest to wait and share your grief in the presence of a counselor. Your counselor or pastor will give you guidance as to the best time to share your hurts with your husband. As you prepare to talk to your husband openly and honestly about the pain he has caused, ask God to use this difficult conversation to fuel his desire for growth and purity. If you are unsure what to share, think about the laments you have poured out to God, then ask yourself the following questions:

- When I grieve my husband's pornography use, what aspect(s) make me saddest?

- What consequences or difficulties has my husband's sin brought upon me (and our children)?

Confronting pornography within a marriage is incredibly difficult for every wife. However, wives of pastors or parachurch ministry leaders face additional hardships. If you are a ministry wife (or your husband is in seminary preparing for ministry), Curtis and I have written appendix 2, "Ministry after Porn," to answer more of your questions.

Questions for Action, Discussion, and Reflection

1. Can you think of a time that your faith was strengthened by watching God work in the life of another believer? (For me, some of life's greatest encouragements have come from watching my friends grow to be more like Jesus.) Share that experience.

2. Where are you in the process of establishing effective accountability? What is the next step you need to take?

3. Can you recall ways that God has used accountability to hold you back from sins that tempt you?

Further Reading on Helping Someone Who Is Battling Pornography

Reju, Deepak, and Jonathan Holmes. *Rescue Plan: Charting a Course to Restore Prisoners of Pornography*. Phillipsburg, NJ: P & R Publishing, 2021.

Reju, Deepak, and Jonathan Holmes. *Rescue Skills: Essential Skills for Restoring the Sexually Broken*. Phillipsburg, NJ: P & R Publishing, 2021.

8

Refuse to Take Revenge

Before you begin this chapter,
please reread 1 Samuel 25:1–35.

THE CONCEPT OF dueling is intriguing. I think of duels as childish fights using very grown-up weapons. Here's a question that I've been pondering lazily since the "Who Shot Alexander Hamilton?" commercial for *Got Milk?* aired in 1993: Why did Aaron Burr shoot Alexander Hamilton? What led two grown men to stand in a field and fire guns at each other? I never took the time to crack open a history book, so I didn't learn the answer until the musical *Hamilton* was performed in my hometown. I am glad I waited because my question was answered in the form of a marvelous experience! It turns out that there were many reasons that duel took place, but betrayal was one of the most significant factors. As we look today at some examples of conflict that arise after betrayal, you will again need to turn your gaze inward and think about ways you have responded to betrayal in your marriage. The spurned lover who seeks revenge is a stereotype for a reason. Vengeance is one common reaction after betrayal—especially by a spouse.

Alexander Hamilton and Aaron Burr's story started out as a friendship. They were young men vying for leadership roles within a newly forming nation. Over many years, their relationship was soured by jealousy and distrust. Eventually they compiled such a large list of grievances that they chose to settle the dispute with a duel. This decision ruined both of their lives. The same could have been true for David and Nabal in 1 Samuel 25 if Abigail hadn't intervened. Neither the conflicts between Alexander and Aaron nor David and Nabal show us the path toward Christlikeness, but they do warn us off the path of revenge. However these men are not the only characters in each story. As much as I looked forward to attending *Hamilton* (and filling in some of the gaps in my knowledge of U.S. history), I did not anticipate that so many months later I would still be thinking about the Hamilton family's story. That's because the brightest star isn't Alexander. It's his wife, Eliza Hamilton. Her servant-hearted fortitude, resiliency, and grace steal the show. We'll look first down the devastating road to revenge before seeking graciousness that we can emulate.

Eliza is the jilted wife in her story. She endured infidelity and public humiliation. Alexander took a mistress, which was soon discovered by that woman's husband. Shockingly, her husband allowed the affair to continue, but he forced Alexander to pay him to keep the situation quiet. Later, when political opponents confronted Hamilton about alleged misuse of funds, Alexander decided to clear his name by publicly circulating a pamphlet explaining that he used his own money to pay that woman's husband for sexual encounters. Eliza responded by burning every letter that Alexander had ever written to her. Her song "Burn" ends with these haunting words to her husband: "I hope you burn."[1]

Have you done anything similar in your marriage? Have you withdrawn from your husband in certain ways amid your pain? That's not always a bad idea. There are circumstances in which withdrawing oneself from the marriage relationship (either temporarily or permanently) are necessary. Whether or not you should engage attentively in the reconciliation process, wait patiently for the outworking of repentance, or separate from your husband are questions best discussed one-on-one with your counselor and pastor. There are situations in which counselors and pastors will counsel a wife to separate. In cases of unrepentant adultery and/or physical, emotional, or sexual abuse, physical separation is not a form of revenge. In these instances, separation is part of the solution—it is meant to keep a wife (and her children) safe while also giving the husband an opportunity to face some of the consequences of his sin toward his family with the hope that he will repent.

As you think through these options and discuss them with a counselor, remember that the heart behind your decision is as significant as the decision itself. David's out-of-proportion response to Nabal shines light on the propensity we all have toward revenge. Both David's and Eliza's reactions should lead us to humbly ask how we can faithfully respond to betrayal. What does faithfulness to God look like when my spouse breaks his marriage covenants and attacks the heart of our union? When vengeance creeps in and I am tempted to direct the thought *I hope you burn!* toward my husband, what should I do? To fully engage with 1 Samuel 25 today, it is important to first understand the relationship between Saul and David, which is recounted in the previous chapters of 1 Samuel.

The relationship between Saul and David started off peacefully. David was a servant in Saul's household. He knew Saul intimately. David played the harp to soothe Saul's nerves when Saul was visited time and again by a tormenting spirit sent from God (1 Samuel 16:14). Sometimes Saul loved David like a son; other times, he tried to kill him. David was able to evade each murderous threat because God's favor rested with him (1 Samuel 18:14). Saul's jealousy mounted as David continually succeeded in military campaigns, his son Jonathan swore allegiance to David, and his daughter Michal fell in love with David. Eventually, Saul began to fear David because he realized that the Lord was with him (1 Samuel 18:28). From that point on, Scripture tells us that "Saul was David's enemy continually" (1 Samuel 18:29).

Even though Saul recognized God's favor toward David, he continued plotting ways to take David's life. During this peril, David was presented with more than one opportunity to kill Saul. Once when Saul was relieving himself in a cave, David sneaked up on him and cut off a corner of his robe. That day David's troops encouraged him to end Saul's life. They claimed that God had given David's enemy into his hand (1 Samuel 24:4). David remained steadfast in the face of this temptation. He rightly believed that Saul has been appointed by God, and he said that killing God's king would be an act of "put[ting] out my hand against my lord, for he is the LORD's anointed" (1 Samuel 24:10). David recognized that vengeance was not his job, and he told Saul that the Lord would have to be the one to avenge any wrongs that Saul had committed (1 Samuel 24:12).

After this, Saul affirmed that David's righteousness surpassed his own, and he declared: "And now, behold, I know that you shall surely be king, and that the kingdom of Israel shall be established in your hand" (1 Samuel 24:20). This picture of David as the self-controlled, future king who waits for God to right every wrong leads into chapter 25. There we learn of David's interaction with Nabal. Given the way he had successfully fended off the temptation to exact revenge against Saul, his response to being slighted by Nabal should take the observant reader by surprise:

> So David's young men turned away and came back and told him all this. And David said to his men, "Every man strap on his sword!" And every man of them strapped on his sword. David also strapped on his sword. And about four hundred men went up after David, while two hundred remained with the baggage. (1 Samuel 25:12–13)

The relationship between Aaron Burr and Alexander Hamilton bears a few striking similarities to the story of Saul and David. We see fierce rivalry and political power at stake, even though

David never let his anger toward Saul come to a head. This is unlike David and Nabal's conflict, which did reach a tipping point and put lives in jeopardy. David and his men had treated Nabal well. David's expectation that his kindness would be returned is understandable, isn't it? Can you relate to this scenario? David had been sinned against unexpectedly. If you have been caught off guard by your husband's pornography use, the temptation toward exacting vengeance is likely more acute than it would be in a situation where you feel prepared to face the sinful actions of another person.

As you read the following applications from this text, please know that the argument I am making here is from lesser to greater. David expected to be compensated for watching over Nabal's herds. It would have been good for Nabal to extend hospitality to David's warriors. But there is no indication that Nabal was contractually obligated to provide for David and his men. However, your expectation of sexual loyalty is fully validated by a marriage covenant. Your husband promised you fidelity. By consuming porn, he has violated specific promises he made on your wedding day. David's anger has been stoked into a consuming blaze by Nabal's slight. If David responds this forcefully to having his unwritten expectations disappointed, how much greater is the temptation toward revenge for a wife whose husband has violated his marriage vows? I would argue that the temptation you face is exponentially greater!

Anger at its worst is a force with the power to destroy (James 4:1–3). As we delve further into this passage, we will arrive at a striking distinction between the course ultimately taken by David and the one charted by Alexander Hamilton. That difference centers around the idea of exacting revenge. As you see the players in these stories respond to betrayal, continue to search yourself for similar tendencies that could lead to either demise or to Christlike flourishing.

David's initial response (v. 13) serves as a warning to any believer who has been betrayed. At the same time that David waited patiently for God to pass the kingship from Saul to himself, his anger flamed into action against his kinsman, Nabal. He gathered his troops for the purpose of annihilating every man in Nabal's household. Even if you haven't been prone to vengeance in the past, carefully guard against this common temptation. David had faithfully demonstrated that God was the one fighting his battles, but at the height of his outrage, he needed a fresh reminder of this truth.

Remember, too, that making a person pay for his actions doesn't always look like strapping on a sword (as it does in this straightforward instance). For every time a woman has responded to sexual betrayal with an adulterous tryst of her own, there has likely been another scenario in which a wife sullenly withdraws her attention from her husband as a way of getting even for the pain he has caused her. Heed the wise counsel of Vicki Tiede, an author whose first husband was an unrepentant pornography user: "Do not be tempted to use the gift (of sexual intimacy) God has given you as a means of wreaking vengeance on your husband."[2] A heart of vengeance could respond in diverse ways—by erupting in rage, by cheating, or by withdrawing. Has your refusal to engage in meaningful dialogue with your spouse resulted in daily exchanges devoid of connection, tenderness, and kindness? Loveless interactions and combative interactions are both forms of retaliation.

Returning to the narrative, let's see how David's vengeful warpath was defused:

> But one of the young men told Abigail, Nabal's wife, "Behold, David sent messengers out of the wilderness to greet our master, and he railed at them. Yet the men were very good to us, and we suffered no harm, and we did not miss anything when we were in the fields, as long as

we went with them. They were a wall to us both by night and by day, all the while we were with them keeping the sheep. Now therefore know this and consider what you should do, for harm is determined against our master and against all his house, and he is such a worthless man that one cannot speak to him."

Then Abigail made haste and took two hundred loaves and two skins of wine and five sheep already prepared and five seahs of parched grain and a hundred clusters of raisins and two hundred cakes of figs, and laid them on donkeys. And she said to her young men, "Go on before me; behold, I come after you." But she did not tell her husband Nabal. And as she rode on the donkey and came down under cover of the mountain, behold, David and his men came down toward her, and she met them. Now David had said, "Surely in vain have I guarded all that this fellow has in the wilderness, so that nothing was missed of all that belonged to him, and he has returned me evil for good. God do so to the enemies of David and more also, if by morning I leave so much as one male of all who belong to him." (1 Samuel 25:14–22)

In their commentary, Carl Friedrich Keil and Franz Delitzsch clarify how David processed Nabal's rude refusal in verses 21–22: "David had said, only for deception (i.e. for no other purpose than to be deceived in my expectation) have I defended all that belongs to this man (Nabal) in the desert, so that nothing of his was missed, and (for) he hath repaid me evil for good."[3]

Lament Your Losses

David thought Nabal was one kind of person, but when he tested those expectations, he discovered Nabal had no intention of reciprocating the kindness he had been shown. Nor did Nabal bestow upon David the honor due God's anointed. Instead, he belittled his nation's next king (v. 10). As a wife who has been betrayed, you can surely relate to having warranted expectations dashed to pieces. Your husband willingly entered marriage. The expectation that he would exhibit sexual integrity is good and reasonable. He also made a commitment to honor you as his bride—and he hasn't. You are processing dismaying information about your husband. He might have hidden this sin from you for a long time. Trying to reconcile who your husband actually is with whom you once believed he was is one of the most painful aspects of discovering that your spouse partakes of pornography.

Take time to lament these discrepancies. Broken trust creates genuine loss. Deception uncovered opens a pitfall of despair because it begs the question, *If this is not true, what else is not true?* To avoid this sinkhole, you will need to cling to Jesus. By doing so, you will be putting into action one of the important truths of 1 Samuel. It takes faith to believe that God will right every wrong. It's a display of trust to wait for the Lord to act on your behalf when you have been sinned against. In a tumultuous moment, David lost sight of this truth.

Wait on the Lord

Waiting on the Lord requires patience, but remember that Abigail didn't confuse patience with passivity. While we wait on the Lord to work, we can still be working for the good of others. Abigail didn't just save her household; she also prevented David from carrying out wicked intentions. In David's response to Abigail, we learn the affects her courageous actions had on him.

> David said to Abigail, "Praise be to the Lord, the God of Israel, who has sent you today to meet me. May you be blessed for your good judgment and for keeping me from bloodshed this day and from avenging myself with my own hands. Otherwise, as surely as the Lord, the God of Israel, lives, who has kept me from harming you, if you

had not come quickly to meet me, not one male belonging to Nabal would have been left alive by daybreak."

Then David accepted from her hand what she had brought him and said, "Go home in peace. I have heard your words and granted your request." (1 Samuel 25:32–35 NIV)

Abigail strengthened her argument against vengeance by reminding David that when believers let God fight their battles, the result is a clear conscience for doing the right thing in the face of evil (v. 32–35). These verses are one of the reasons that I asked you to read this book alongside a faithful friend. You have been deeply wounded by your closest companion, your husband. In the days and weeks to come, you may need this same reminder if the temptation to take revenge rears its ugly head. Abigail served David by proclaiming truth to him. She prevented him from causing irreversible damage and bringing upon himself all the shame and guilt that would have ensued had he carried out his plan. Commit to telling your friend anytime the temptation to take revenge strikes. Ask her to promise to point you toward relevant truth if you begin to stray.

We saw Abigail's determination to bring about whatever good she could when she wisely mediated peace between David and her household. Eliza Hamilton (another hero of mine) also demonstrates wisdom through her actions.

In the final years of his life, Alexander reconciled with Eliza. He began attending church with her and they were sighted walking together around the city. But he didn't make peace with Aaron Burr. Alexander Hamilton and Aaron Burr's conflict ended with a duel at Weehawken. Their rivalry finally resolved when Alexander died from a bullet wound.

Eliza's story ended much differently. The most beautiful moments of *Hamilton* come in the final song. Vengeance quenched her husband's life, but Eliza's remaining years exuded grace. Alexander was silenced by his rage. So Eliza gets the last word. At the crescendo of this musical, she sings, "I put myself back in the narrative."

From my seat in the theater, with tears streaming down my face, I contemplated her legacy. In the musical, for a time she withdrew herself from the story, but she later reengaged. She outlived her husband by fifty years. During that time, she embodied selfless, public service. Eliza raised funds for the Washington Monument, spoke against slavery, and opened the first private orphanage in New York City. There she cared for hundreds of orphans as a tribute to Alexander, who had been orphaned at a young age.[4]

All of this good came out of Eliza's decision to put aside retribution and instead model proactive love. It is my hope that the examples of Eliza and Abigail help you put off vengeance and discover the answer to this question: What would it look like for me to put myself back in the narrative?

Questions for Action, Discussion, and Reflection

1. Have you been tempted to seek revenge against your husband? By your actions have you tried to make him continually pay for what he has done? If so, what forms did your desire for revenge take?

2. What would it look like for you to put yourself back in the narrative?

3. Anger often fuels the desire for revenge. What does Proverbs 29:11 say about responding out of anger?

Further Reading on Anger

Powlison, David. *Good and Angry: Redeeming Anger, Irritation, Complaining, and Bitterness.* Greensboro, NC: New Growth Press, 2016.

9

Mercy for the Sexually Broken

Before you begin this chapter, please read Luke 7:36–50.

IN YOUR PREVIOUS study of Scripture, has Jesus ever surprised you? Have his words or actions disquieted your view of reality enough that your perspective changed? Has he ever awakened new, holy desires in you that made the sinful pleasures you once craved seem unappealing? Has he ever convicted you of sin and brought you to repentance? If the answer to these questions is yes, do you believe that he can do the same for your husband?

Christians grow in Christlikeness. As believers cultivate godly desires, they will see patterns of sin change into new rhythms of holiness (albeit slowly and imperfectly). Faith-filled living isn't static; it's dynamic. Therefore, the moment of salvation isn't the only time God surprises his children with new perspectives. The ongoing work of sanctification is full of these moments.

These opportunities to draw closer to God often come when we submit our minds and hearts to Scripture. Some passages will attend us like a healing balm. Others will chafe like sandpaper, tearing callouses off our hearts. At times God's word will also reveal sin we didn't know was present. Ask God to grant you a humble heart that willingly accepts Scripture's comfort and its rebukes. Ask God to do the same for your husband. Healing comes through both channels.

Today we are going to look at the historical account of a sexual sinner who repents and bestows on Jesus love that is greater than it would have been if she had never sinned sexually. Did that sentence make you scratch your head and wonder if you are reading the right book? This book is written for people who have been deeply wounded by the sexual sin of a spouse. Why in the world would I broach this subject here and now? That's a fair question, and I will try to answer it before we dive into the story.

Healing Is Possible

I want us to study this passage together because Jesus can and does heal sexual brokenness. Most people who struggle with pornography and other sexual sins don't just sin once in this area. Some people never repent, and for the ones who do, the journey toward Christlikeness is often two steps forward, one step back. I bet you've experienced this faltering growth too. Take a look back at the sin struggles in your own life to see if there's a similar pattern. Granted, understanding from experience that sanctification is a slow process doesn't make finding out that your spouse has viewed pornography (or has *yet again* viewed pornography) any less painful, and that is assuming he is repentant and growing. The pain only increases for a woman who is married to an unbelieving husband who, thus far, probably hasn't expressed any genuine desire to change and grow. That same pain is compounded by confusion for a woman married to a man who professes faith in Christ and either isn't repentant or says he's repentant without exhibiting any visible change. In all these situations, the pain of dealing with porn creates a temptation toward hopelessness. Have you experienced hopeless thoughts about your husband, such as *He's never going to change* or *God's never going to use him now—he's ruined everything*? As we explore this text today, you'll have an opportunity to meditate on God's great mercy toward a repentant sexual sinner. Ask God to allow his great mercy to increase your hope through the truth that Jesus is more than able to heal sexual brokenness.

In Luke 7:36–50, Jesus accepts the worship of a former prostitute. This is good news for us and our marriages! God can and does change sexual sinners. Even if you have waited a long time without seeing any signs of growth in your husband's life, God can still bring him to repentance. The woman at the center of today's story has been transformed by God's grace. Imagining her history will magnify the trustworthiness of Jesus. She was shunned and unwelcome in polite society while being sought after continually as a means of cheap pleasure—living in a duality fit for despair. Surely this life filled with loveless interactions left her distrusting toward men.

Contending with Brokenness

Are there ways you can relate to her story? Weeping gratefully at the feet of Jesus may be a familiar position to you if you have been forgiven the heavy burden of your own sexual sin (or any other sin). Perhaps you bear the scars of sexual brokenness that was imposed on you by the choices of another person. If you have been disciplined in avoiding sexual sins and have also been protected from the abusive sexual advances of others, it could just as easily feel foreign to encounter this prostitute's world. It's also possible that you might be so deeply entrenched in legalism that you can't imagine grace that applies to sexual sin. *Suffering* is the word that best describes the circumstances that brought most readers to this book. Have you been badly wounded by your husband's choices but still remain deeply committed to responding as Jesus does to your husband's sexual sin and brokenness? Whatever the case may be, this parable will speak to you.

Let's pretend we had the opportunity to attend this tense dinner party. Which character do you most relate to in the story— the judgmental host; the broken, repentant sexual sinner; or the amazed onlookers? God's word will go to work on you differently depending on your answer. It could have a convicting rebuke or a tender encouragement for you today. Either way, if you respond humbly to Jesus, his grace will buoy you with hope.

Scripture Is Unchanging

Before we take a seat at Simon's table, we need a moment to remember Jesus's stance toward sexual sin. He has clear expectations regarding sexual expression. Let's take a brief look at one of the passages we explore in appendix 3, "Is Pornography Use Grounds for Divorce": "You have heard that it was said, 'You shall not commit adultery. But I say to you that everyone who looks at a woman with lustful intent has already committed adultery with her in his heart" (Matthew 5:27–28). Even as our contemporary society throws off sexual restraints, the ethic of Scripture remains unmovable, exactly the same as it has been for thousands of years. Broadening the borders of allowable sexual expression won't heal your marriage; it will only lead to deeper wounds. Jesus's words affirm rigid parameters around sexual experiences. We are accountable for our sexually motivated actions, for all our sexual thoughts, and for every type of sexual expression that falls in between. Your husband's pornography use doesn't receive a "get out of jail free" pass from Jesus. So it shouldn't get one from you either.

Sexual fidelity has unchanging parameters, but the porn industry is constantly expanding its array of enticements. Internet technology has set recent precedents that were unheard of through most of human history—explicit images can now be exchanged easily and anonymously. Lust has always been a struggle for fallen people, but lust hasn't always had the option to consult an unending visual buffet of paid actors at its leisure. Ubiquitous internet access has removed prohibitive social roadblocks. The danger is also heightened by the porn industry's predatory pursuit of people. First it learns a user's preferences, and then it crafts uniquely targeted temptations. The people making porn lure and enslave people for money. They profit by debilitating men and women, both outside the church and within it. As smart technology becomes more sophisticated, this effective predation is likely to increase.

God's Mercy

All this to say, there isn't an easy road out of the pain you are facing. The influx of obscene images is real. The temptation to view those images is real. Choosing to view porn is a blatant sin. This suffering you are experiencing as a result of your husband's choices is real. And the same Jesus who calls porn a sin loves a prostitute! God's mercy exceeds all expectations. Are you ready for that? If so, let's join Jesus now. He's dining at the home of Simon the Pharisee:

> One of the Pharisees asked [Jesus] to eat with him, and [Jesus] went into the Pharisee's house and took his place at the table. And behold, a woman of the city, who was a sinner, when she learned that [Jesus] was reclining at the table in the Pharisee's house, brought an alabaster flask of ointment, and standing behind [Jesus] at his feet, weeping, she began to wet his feet with her tears and wiped them with the hair of her head and kissed his feet and anointed them with the ointment. (Luke 7:36–38)

Jesus preached in many towns during his public ministry. It was common for guest speakers to be invited to someone's home for a meal after a time of public teaching. These meals often took place in outdoor courtyards and sometimes included further teaching by the visiting rabbi, along with questions from the crowd.[1] These were not exclusive, invitation-only events in the way that dinner parties usually are today. People from the town were welcome to enter the courtyard and stand around the table listening.[2] In many ways, this gathering at Simon the Pharisee's home represents this typical type of banquet.

While Jesus reclines at Simon's dinner table, a former prostitute enters the courtyard. Her mere presence immediately disquieted an otherwise normal gathering. Pharisees were scrupulous about ritual purity, especially while eating. Prostitutes were ritually unclean.[3] To complicate things further, a respectable man (let alone a religious leader) would never allow a morally disreputable woman to touch him. This is not a surprising historical insight. Two thousand years later, an uninvited prostitute is still not a welcome addition at any dinner party. To make matters worse, the woman lets her hair down. During the time the New Testament was written, honorable women did not wear their hair loose. It was such a serious offense that Jewish law said a Jewish man could divorce his wife for letting her hair down in public.[4] A woman who chose to breach this social contract was easily distinguishable as promiscuous.

Initially, this woman's actions might have been open to misinterpretation, but as events unfold it's clear that she isn't being provocative. The same hairstyle that once drew attention to her sexual availability is here being used solely as an expression of reverence. The kisses she previously used to entice men are now reflecting her humble devotion to Jesus. We see this theme repeated in the ointment. It was likely carried in a small vial on a necklace. Women commonly used it as both perfume and breath freshener.[5] It's easy to see how this would be an important addition to a prostitute's work. She is employing three of her most alluring assets, but they have been transformed into means of bringing honor to the Lord. This passage demonstrates something important about repentance. It is bound up inextricably with worship and humility. Do you pray regularly for your husband's sexual purity? Pray, also, that your husband would be humble and intent upon worshiping Jesus.

This former prostitute has every reason to walk through the world with all her guards up until she encounters grace so compelling that it empowers her to trust God. In order to come close to Jesus, she must throw caution to the wind, cast off social conventions, and ignore the contempt of the religious leaders who despise her. We find her dropping all her defenses in a most unlikely place because she is singularly focused on drawing near to Jesus. She is willing to express risky, vulnerable, lavish worship for one reason—she trusts Jesus, the one who is completely worthy of her attentive affection. The unhindered devotion of the woman with the alabaster flask is surprising, but another aspect of this interaction is far more astounding. Let's turn our attention to the way Jesus responds to her affection. Her actions are noteworthy, yet they point to a Savior who is even more remarkable.

Jesus doesn't follow pharisaical social protocols. It's clear that he is impervious to peer pressure. He doesn't insist that the woman be escorted out of the courtyard. He doesn't try to smooth things over, reiterate his own moral purity, or even apologize for the perceived disruption. God didn't put on flesh to help Simon (or me, or you) maintain the facade of your family's public image. He's not interested in helping us pull off the perfect dinner party. He came to earth to bring glory to God the Father by redeeming sinners. Watch as he turns this uncomfortable gathering into an opportunity to teach Simon (and us) something important about himself.

First, Jesus welcomes the woman! Her interruption of the status quo is not inconvenient to our savior. He allows her to come close. He knows her repentance is genuine. He accepts her worship. The language Jesus uses later indicates that her sins had been forgiven on a previous occasion (v. 47). She encountered the gospel and received new life prior to this evening. She is not here trying to earn favor with Jesus. Rather, she is expressing gratitude for the love and mercy that he has already freely extended to her.[6] Jesus receives her unapologetically. He doesn't ask her to step outside and wait until he finishes the final course. Our savior unabashedly welcomes forgiven sinners.

This unexpected series of events illuminates truths that will be formative as you seek Jesus in the aftermath of your husband's sin. First, Jesus never disparages women. Society treated this broken, sinful woman like a disposable object. Jesus valued her and wanted her to come close. Jesus loves women perfectly. You have made the painful discovery that your husband is not trustworthy. To an extent this is true for all spouses, not just those who have experienced betrayal. Your heart is not ultimately safe with your husband. It is only perfectly safe with Jesus.

Here's something else that's clear from the passage: Jesus welcomes repentant sinners, including sexually immoral sinners. Is there unconfessed sexual sin in your past or present? You can confess it to Jesus. In order to grow in Christlikeness, you must confess and forsake it. When you do, he will forgive you. Contrite sinners and wounded sufferers who cast themselves at the feet of Jesus are always received. He embraces the wayward, brokenhearted, and mistreated alike. There is still a way for you to get to him today. He has done all the work. If you have already trusted him by faith, then he lived and died for you, called you, and equipped you. If you don't yet know him, come to him without delay (Romans 10:9)! Let today be the day of your salvation (2 Corinthians 6:2). He is the only person who will never disappoint you.

In addition to your need for Christ's mercy, there is another way you can relate to the prostitute who anointed Jesus's feet. If your husband struggles with pornography, his divided interest has brought you a similar weight of rejection. Have you experienced the confusion of feeling simultaneously sought after and cast off by your husband? When he pursues you, do you ever feel like you are just one of many available means to the ends of his sexual gratification? Or maybe he has rejected your physical affection completely. Has he abandoned marital intimacy altogether, instead seeking pleasure solely through porn? The woman in this story is acquainted with the distress of rejection. She displays wisdom by drawing near to the one whose affections are never divided.

In the next scene of this story, the interaction between Jesus and Simon offers a stark contrast:

> When the Pharisee who had invited him saw this, he said to himself, "If this man were a prophet, he would have known who and what sort of woman this is who is touching him, for she is a sinner." And Jesus answering said to him, "Simon, I have something to say to you." And he answered, "Say it, teacher." (Luke 7:39–40)

Simon makes an utterly hopeless mental assessment of the scene, but he doesn't verbalize it; verse 39 is sharing Simon's thoughts. This is a comforting truth that's worth revisiting. Because Jesus is God, he knows Simon's thoughts! Jesus also knows every thought (and every hidden action) of every person who has ever lived. If your husband has repented, Jesus has welcomed him to come close and has accepted his tears as worship. Have you found yourself thinking thoughts like Simon's: *If Jesus knew what kind of man my husband is, he wouldn't embrace such a sinner!* If this is true, you must remember that Jesus knows your husband better than anyone. Sadly, Simon wasn't willing to see the beauty of grace. He was blind to God's work in this woman even as it blossomed in his own home. What about you? Do you still hope for God to bring about repentance and real change? Pray often for eyes to see the transformation that Jesus can surely create in your husband, if or when he repents.

Coming into the Light

Have you noticed that you learn more about yourself and others in the uncomfortable moments of life than the moments when everything is going as planned? There's a unique way that difficulty reveals carefully hidden parts of us. The awkwardness of tense interactions can bring to light the best parts of us and the parts of us that need to be sanctified. Just as God was being gracious to your husband when he brought his porn use to light, God is also showing you kindness when he reveals areas of your life that need to change. Do you, like Simon, lack a hopeful heart?

To reveal Simon's heart, Jesus tells a parable. This story reaches its crescendo in the next three verses. In response to the events that have transpired, Jesus says,

> "A certain moneylender had two debtors. One owed five hundred denarii, and the other fifty. When they could not pay, he cancelled the debt of both. Now which of them will love him more?" Simon answered, "The one, I suppose, for whom he cancelled the larger debt." And [Jesus] said to [Simon], "You have judged rightly." (Luke 7:41–43)

Since these words come from the same Jesus who decisively teaches that lust is a sin, we can be certain that this parable does not let anyone off the hook for sexual sin. Rather, this passage speaks about the effect that forgiveness has on a repentant soul: A moneylender forgives the debts of two people. One owes a great sum and the other owes a much smaller amount. Not all sin debts are exactly equal. There are greater sin debts and lesser sin debts. Even so, both debtors in the story owe much more than they can repay. This is always the case with our sin debts before God. Regardless of whether your sin debt is smaller or larger than your neighbor's, you still owe God far more than you could ever pay back. See the great mercy of the moneylender! After both debts are completely canceled, which person does Jesus say will love the moneylender more? What does this passage tell us about the person who comes to Jesus and repents of great sin? Jesus tells us that receiving a greater measure of forgiveness will result in a greater measure of love.

Has your history of chaste behavior led you to believe that sexually immoral people are beyond hope? Have you worried that your repentant husband will always remain a second-class Christian because of his past sexual sin? Has your husband's blatant unrepentance caused you to give up hope that he will ever turn back to Jesus? His story is not over yet. Neither is yours. With Jesus there is great hope and abundant mercy for repentant sexual sinners.

How do the ironic ramifications of this parable impact you? If Simon had known the depths of his own sin, he too would have been weeping at the feet of Jesus, because that's where all of us belong. But the Pharisee remained unmoved by his encounter with the one who has the power to forgive sins. Don't follow suit. Allow yourself to experience grace and hope in the presence of Jesus. The sexually immoral person who recognizes the depth of their sin and repents will be welcomed by Jesus and will pour out upon Jesus lavish love and affection. Isn't this astounding? This is the type of grace-filled paradigm shift that only a merciful God can bring forth. You might be tempted to believe that your husband's choices (or your own) have spoiled his (or your) chances of ever serving God again. Yet this parable tells us that if repentance is part of the equation, both of you are far from being ruined. If your husband admits the depth of his depravity and accepts Jesus's merciful provision, then extraordinary grace could ignite within him a deep and profound love for his Savior.

Can you see the sweeping abundance of God's mercy? Will you hope for this type of transformation in your husband? Immense grace produces bountiful love. And that grace is available to all, including the sexually broken. This is a staggering, hope-inspiring promise of the gospel.

Questions for Action, Discussion, and Reflection

1. Did anything about today's verses surprise you? If so, what?

2. Is there unrepentant sexual sin in your life? If so, are you willing to confess your guilt to Jesus and ask him for forgiveness?

3. Have you believed that past sexual sin will always stand between you and Jesus? If you have repented of that sin, what does this passage say to you?

4. What are the implications of Luke 7:36–50 for others (including your husband) who repent of sexual sin?

5. Some people who read this passage might wrongly believe that they should go on sinning more in order to eventually have greater love for God. What does Romans 6:1–2 say in response to this idea? For more helpful thoughts on this, watch John Piper's explanation in Look at the Book, Luke 7:36–50, Part 2, "God's Love for the Worst."[7]

6. The woman with the alabaster flask used her hair, perfume, and tears to worship Jesus. What would it look like for you to demonstrate your desperate need for Jesus and your love for Him?

7. If you've had hopeless thoughts toward your husband, name them. How does this passage speak to them? Can you think of additional Bible verses that counter feelings of hopelessness?

Further Reading

Powlison, David. *Making All Things New: Restoring Joy to the Sexually Broken*. Wheaton, IL: Crossway, 2017.

10

Willing to Welcome?

NOT EVERY BROKEN relationship ends in reconciliation. The question, *Are you willing to welcome?* comes from me to you with that reality in mind. I experienced the repercussions of two divorces before my eighteenth birthday. There was no reconciliation in either situation, as my family splintered and reformed, only to splinter and reform again. My adopted dad (who was my mom's second husband) remained present as a father in my life after they divorced during my teen years. My biological father didn't. He battled addictions and was only available to parent me on a few summer vacations before my tenth birthday. After that, I only saw him one more time before his death nearly twenty years later. Some relationships break permanently.

I don't know the trajectory your marriage will take, but as we discuss forgiveness, you will notice that I haven't included any time frames. That's intentional. The precise when and how of forgiveness need to be talked through with someone who knows what the Bible says about forgiveness, knows the details of your situation, and has had a chance to observe your husband's demonstrations of repentance (or his lack of true repentance) over time. Many marriages that are damaged by porn can and should be reconciled, but this is not the case in every instance (particularly in cases where there is illegal porn use, abusive porn use, or unrepentant porn use that escalates into other forms of sexual sin). When reconciliation can and does happen, it's a beautiful testimony to God's grace and can result in a marriage that's better and stronger than ever. This true healing can happen if the spouse who has sinned sexually is humble and repentant before the Lord and before his or her spouse, and if the spouse who was sinned against is committed to extending grace and forgiveness in an ongoing way. That's why the question, *Are you willing to welcome?* is so important.

Forgiving Is Welcoming

One of the most basic manifestations of forgiveness is the willing extension of a warm welcome. That's why we are going to take another look at Luke 7:36–50. Here Simon misses an opportunity to welcome Jesus. He is also unwilling to extend forgiveness to a woman who has repented of sexual sin. Neither of these is surprising, given that Simon hadn't encountered the transforming grace of God. The same should not be said of a person who has a relationship with Christ. Once we have been received by Jesus, we are instructed to welcome others who repent. I don't want you to miss the opportunity to welcome your husband warmly if he turns from his sin. Are you ready for this? If not, this chapter will help you prepare.

Once when I hosted a playdate, a toddler exhibited MacGyver-level creativity. He turned the pointy edge of his Lego creation into a writing implement and etched our big-screen television with scrawling loops and scribbles. The damage was permanent and noticeable. Our TV bears the marks of hospitality. This boy has since moved to another city, and we don't see him regularly. I realized soon after he moved that I think about him every time I walk past our TV. So I put this reminder to good use. Each time I notice the scratches, I pray for him. I pray for this child more regularly than any others, except my own.

We all expect that preschoolers will make messes, but what happens when the destructive person in your life is your husband? He's supposed to be mature and trustworthy. He's the man who has pledged to love you until death. What happens when he has shattered something that isn't trivial like a TV screen—instead he has broken your trust in him? When he turns to porn, that's what gets broken. Holding on to possessions loosely is one thing. The expectation that the love we express toward a spouse will always be reciprocated with loving-kindness is much harder to relinquish. Scratched TVs can be lived with or replaced. Broken promises result in broken hearts, which are infinitely more precious and exponentially harder to mend. Moving forward, there are bound to be recurring painful reminders of the past. When your attention is drawn toward the scars, take time to lament the pain, and then allow those memories to become profitable opportunities to pray for your husband.

Offering a warm welcome after someone repents is not possible without a heart that is willing to also extend forgiveness, but forgiving someone isn't the same thing as trusting them. Would I have offered my preschool friend forgiveness had he asked for it? Absolutely. Would I have given the same child unsupervised access to my home in the near future? No. Forgiving releases a person from the sin debt that he owes you, but it doesn't mean you should unreservedly trust him in all the ways you once did. The next time that child visited my home I stayed in the room while he played with Legos. If he hadn't moved away, I would have cautiously watched for growth and maturity before allowing him to play unaccompanied by an adult. The same is true for your marriage. If your husband repents, you will need to forgive him and welcome him in a way that makes space for him to begin rebuilding your trust. But this doesn't mean that you are expected to relate to him exactly the same way you did before you became aware of his porn use. He misused your trust in a way that demonstrates spiritual immaturity. Extending a welcome should be done wisely, accounting for the pain you are experiencing and the ways he's prone to temptation.

Can you think of ways you can begin to welcome him as he works to demonstrate willingness to act in consistent, mature, and dependable ways? Here are two ways that come to mind— please add your own to the list: Would you be willing to pray out loud with him, asking God to work in your marriage? Would you be open to letting him plan a date night to discuss some of the things that God has been teaching each of you recently? Start slow. A warm welcome doesn't mean acting like everything is back to normal. It is deliberately making time for relational connection points that can build over time as he manifests a life set on pleasing God and loving you well.

A person with a welcoming heart is willing to risk potential hardship because only in a home where forgiveness is practiced can sinners grow and flourish. As you bring yourself before our passage in Luke today, keep in mind these questions: (a) What does Simon's example teach us about forgiveness? (b) How can I cultivate a life that extends a warm welcome to repentant, struggling people?

Let's revisit Simon's inner monologue: "When the Pharisee who had invited him saw this, he said to himself, 'If this man were a prophet, he would know who is touching him and what kind of woman she is—that she is a sinner'" (Luke 7:39 NIV). Now remember, Jesus isn't a party crasher in this story. Simon invited Jesus to dinner. However, an invitation isn't the same thing as a welcome. Jesus is a guest, yet Simon offers him a cold reception. He doubts Jesus's ability to discern the hearts of people, and he is skeptical of Jesus's status as a prophet.

As the evening progresses, it becomes clear that self-righteous Simon is also unwilling to receive the one who has repented of sin and earnestly wants to grow. Jesus declared that the woman who anointed his feet was forgiven. Yet when Simon looked at her, all he could see were the sins she once committed. Have you likewise exhibited a self-righteous attitude toward your husband? It may have manifested in thoughts like these: *I am a much better Christian than he is; if other people knew the ways he has sinned, they wouldn't accept him.* If so, it will be instructive to take a hard look at the responses of this prideful religious leader.

In the next several verses, Jesus will point out Simon's failure to extend an appropriate welcome. We can see from verse 39 that these examples point to a grave deficit in his life. Simon's lack of faith in Jesus has overflowed into actions. Have you seen similar evidence of unbelief in your own life? Do you find yourself doubting Jesus is who he says he is? Have you disbelieved God's goodness because the circumstances in your marriage are difficult? Your thoughts will likewise flow into actions.

Giving lip service to Jesus's status is not the same thing as accepting his authority. Kenneth Bailey draws attention to this truth from Luke 7:40: "Simon indirectly confesses his own failures as a host by addressing Jesus with the title Rabbi/Teacher. If he is worthy of the title that Simon grants to him, then he is worthy of the honor due the title, but this honor Simon withholds from him."[1] Do you say that Jesus is the creator, sustainer, and king of the universe? Do you treat him as though he is the creator, sustainer, and king of your home? If you are not worshiping him as he deserves, what would it look like for you to begin to honor Jesus?

Verses 44-46 speak about the importance of our actions. Your husband may have wrecked your trust by lying. At the point he chose to speak deceptively, his words lost their solidity. They became mirages—vague glimmers on the horizon that provide no assurance because they do not represent reality. When Jesus rebukes Simon, he highlights Simon's actions. That's because these are the most accurate display of what Simon believes about Jesus. In the days to come, your husband's words will hold much less weight than his actions. His repentance toward God, coupled with loving, humble responses toward you, will become the building blocks that can slowly rebuild trust.

Serving Is Welcoming

Let us return to the narrative and read Jesus's pointed rebuke: "Then turning toward the woman [Jesus] said to Simon, 'Do you see this woman? I entered your house; you gave me no water for my feet, but she has wet my feet with her tears and wiped them with her hair'" (Luke 7:44). Imagine the scene at this Middle Eastern dinner party. Guests dined reclining on their left sides. They would prop themselves up on the left elbow and keep their feet pointing away from the table.[2] In wealthier households, a servant would come by with a basin, a pitcher of water, and a towel in order to rinse and dry the guest's soiled feet.[3]

Scripture returns to the theme of foot washing several times to indicate expressions of honor and humility. Simon's decision not to tend Jesus's feet is (at best) an indication that he believes he is superior to Jesus.[4] The forgiven woman approaches Jesus humbly, using her hair (which Paul refers to as a woman's glory in 1 Corinthians 11:15) to anoint his feet. John the Baptist shows reverence by confessing that he is not worthy to untie Jesus's sandals in Luke 3:16.[5] At the last supper, we see foreshadowing of Jesus's voluntary death on the cross when he serves his disciples by washing their feet. At Simon's house we see more of Jesus's humility. He does not point out to Simon that someone should have washed his feet. Instead, Jesus says that he would have washed his own feet, but Simon did not provide him any water. Jesus's meek response to his disdainful host provides a stark contrast to Simon's prideful discourtesy.

Expanding sexual expression beyond marital intimacy is arrogant. By doing this, your husband has dishonored God and you. In addition to using porn, there may be other ways that he has been disrespectful and inhospitable toward you. How do you think about your rights within marriage? Have you demanded them? Jesus said he came to serve rather than to be served (Matthew 20:28). What would it look like for you to follow his example? Are you willing to look for opportunities to follow Jesus by laying aside your rights? While it is important for all wives, myself included, to think this through, it is equally important to note that I am not encouraging submitting to abuse. If your husband is asserting himself in any ways that indicate abuse, please read appendix 1, "Porn and Abuse." Welcoming an abusive spouse is not loving; it is enabling him to continue sinning. If abuse is a piece of your story, you will find information in that appendix that is readily applicable to your marriage.

Next, Jesus says to Simon, "You gave me no kiss, but from the time I came in she has not ceased to kiss my feet" (Luke 7:45). Offering a kiss was a traditional sign of welcome. Again, Simon's omission here is a poignant one. Rabbis were honored guests so they were received with the utmost respect. Here's a description of this deferential greeting: "In the case of a Rabbi, all the male members of the family wait at the entrance of the house and kiss his hands."[6] Kissing a person on the cheek showed respect as an equal. Kissing someone's hand was a way of acknowledging his status as greater than your own.[7] Kissing a person's feet was not customary. Only a person trying to indicate the greatest measure of humility in the presence of someone to whom they owed a great debt would bestow kisses on feet.[8]

Here Jesus draws another contrast between the actions of Simon and the woman: "You did not anoint my head with oil, but she has anointed my feet with ointment" (Luke 7:46). Oil in this passage is a reference to inexpensive olive oil. Jesus contrasts this everyday staple with the costly perfume employed by the forgiven woman.[9] Again, Jesus does not demand extravagant treatment from Simon. His indictments press no further than Simon's failure to offer basic accommodations. Imagine if Jesus had brought the full force of his charges against Simon. It might have been something like this:

> I am the author of the universe, Simon. In me all things hold together. Each breath you breathe is air that I made—drawn into lungs that I knit together while you were helpless in your mother's womb, yet you choose not to greet me with respect? You refuse to welcome me even though all that you are and all that you have are gracious gifts from my hand!

Jesus could have said all this and much more, yet his restraint here shows us his nature. God's kindness leads us to repentance (Romans 2:4). You might feel as though speaking the full weight of your husband's sins aloud to him will be the only way for him to see the depths of his depravity, but the example of Jesus shows another possibility. Jesus is winsome and gives restrained examples meant to point Simon to his deepest need—forgiveness of sin. Jesus is willing to lay aside his rights to give Simon an opportunity to repent. Jesus speaks here not to vindicate himself, but to convict Simon. His words are spoken in love—for Simon's benefit.

While Jesus's rebuke towards Simon is relatively restrained, these next few sentences from Jesus might seem excessive: "'Therefore I tell you, her sins, which are many, are forgiven—for she loved much. But he who is forgiven little, loves little.' And he said to her, 'Your sins are forgiven'" (Luke 7:47–48). Maybe you have worked hard your whole life to maintain sexual purity. If so, it might be tempting to feel nothing but reproach toward your husband's sexual sin. Simon, the Pharisee, clearly regarded the woman anointing Jesus with disgust. As you sort through your responses to pornography, this common temptation could arise. None of us are immune to pride. Self-righteousness is a dangerous form of pride that can feel justifiable. After all, you are the one who has been sinned against. Have you been tempted to make mental lists of all the things you have done right in your marriage, including all the ways you have loved your family well or served the church? That list might be followed by all the ways your husband has failed, deceived you, and disregarded your affection. It is important that you watch your broken heart carefully. Wounds can fester, and when this happens your heart can quickly become infected with sin that will be all your own. Simon shows us what happens when a person closes his heart to God's grace.

Open doors and open hearts are vulnerable places. Even people with the best intentions can't help but bring along their sin. Believers display the gospel to others by fostering a hospitable environment where sinners can repent, live, and grow. Forgiveness is essential to the type of hospitality that brings about relational flourishing. As much as I would love to be done with my sin and live perfectly the rest of my days on earth, I am a fallen person. I will continue to fight against sin until I reach heaven. As much as I am dependent on God's continued forgiveness (and the grace he grants me to humbly seek the forgiveness of my family and friends), my spouse will likewise continue to struggle with his own sin—whether it is lust or something else—and will also need ongoing forgiveness.

It's also true that forgiveness is a transaction. We don't receive forgiveness from Jesus until we ask him for it. Your husband will need to take part in this exchange. To gain forgiveness (from God and you), he must confess his sin and repent of it (1 John 1:9). Have you ever had the opportunity to forgive your husband for his porn use? How did it go? You might be praying right now that he would confess his sin and repent for the first time. Does the thought of getting to forgive him bring you joy? Perhaps it does. If so, rejoice that God has tuned your heart to give grace to others. If not, let Simon's example motivate your resolve to learn to forgive. If we don't prime our hearts, we will disobey God and miss out on the joy that comes from receiving a repentant sinner.

Remembering God's Forgiveness toward You Leads to Welcoming

Have you ever attempted to forgive someone and found that you were unable to let go of the grudge you held against him? Have you ever wondered if God is holding a grudge against you? That's because there is an immeasurable distance between your heart and God's. Forgiveness is a gift that God loves to give! Mercy is at the heart of God's character. In Exodus 34:6–7 God describes himself as "merciful and gracious, slow to anger, and abounding in steadfast love and faithfulness, keeping steadfast love for thousands, forgiving iniquity and transgression and sin, but who will by no means clear the guilty." Dane Ortlund gives a beautiful description of the way this passage shows us God's desire to forgive:

> Not once are we told that God is "provoked to love" or "provoked to mercy." His anger requires provocation; his mercy is pent up, ready to gush forth. We tend to think: divine anger is pent up, spring-loaded; divine mercy is slow to build. It's just the opposite. Divine mercy is ready to burst forth at the slightest prick. (For fallen humans, we learn in the New Testament, this is reversed. We are to provoke one another to love, according to Hebrews 10:24. Yahweh needs no provoking to love, only to anger. We need no provoking to anger, only to love....)[10]

The second that we forget our own need for Jesus's forgiveness and start racking up a mental list of personal merits is also the second that we forget the truth that apart from God we can do nothing (John 15:5). Every single good thing you have ever done, including any sexual purity, self-control, and steadfastness, is a result of God's grace. You can't take credit for your good works. Owning the truth of the gospel makes it impossible to look at others with contempt because we all need grace.

In addition to this, Jesus commands forgiveness. The sin debt that you have been forgiven by God is far greater than the sin debt your husband owes you. Commenting on Matthew 18:21–35, which is known as "the parable of the unforgiving servant," Robert Jones says, "Jesus then makes his unmistakable point, the point of the parable: we who have been forgiven a mega-debt should forgive others from our hearts. 'This is how my Heavenly Father will treat each of you unless you forgive your brother from your heart' (v. 35). Failing to forgive invites severe consequences."[11]

Simon was not the only one at that dinner party who struggled to grasp God's grace: "Then those who were at table with him began to say among themselves, 'Who is this, who even forgives sins?' And he said to the woman, 'Your faith has saved you; go in peace'" (Luke 7:49–50). There is no lasting peace apart from Jesus. Sexual sin is fraught with trauma, shame, and despair. While a person remains enslaved to sin, they will not experience peace. When David wrestled with his sins toward Bathsheba and Uriah, he said his bones wasted away within him (Psalm 32:3). As you pray for your husband this week, ask God to bring him the peace that comes only through reconciliation to God.

Did you notice the response of the other guests at Simon's dinner party? After watching Jesus interact with this woman they said, "Who is this, who even forgives sins?" (v. 49). This same question could be asked in disbelief or with a tone of glad amazement. If you were dining at Simon's table that night, how would that question have proceeded from your lips? Now picture your husband as the one kneeling before Jesus. Would you (like Simon) have derided Jesus's lavish attention toward the penitent, or would you have rejoiced to see the exchange?

Showing Grace Is Welcoming

God is at work in each of his children, equipping them to extend costly grace to others. He knows better than anyone the steep price of warmly welcoming sinners. If forgiving your husband still seems too painful, ask him for help. You can approach him because you are the recipient of grace that left Jesus with permanent scars (John 20:27). Because God gave his only son, he can forgive and welcome you. In turn, he asks you to paint grace and forgiveness on the canvas of your husband's heart, even while your life bears painful reminders of the sin he has committed. If your spouse hasn't yet repented, then Christlike love will cause you to pray eagerly for that day to come.

Over the years I have had many opportunities to grant (and ask for!) forgiveness, but God hasn't yet completed his work in me. There are times when giving forgiveness proves difficult. I am still learning what it means to extend a warm welcome to those who have sinned against me. Have you already envisioned what it might look like to warmly welcome your husband? If not, try to think of one grace-filled step in his direction, a loving gesture that communicates to him that all is not lost and that through Jesus you still hold out hope that there can be relational healing. When forgiveness feels costly and painful, I find it helpful to imagine grace in action. And there is one image that comes to my mind—it's a man in a hospital gown drinking a chocolate peanut butter milkshake.

Two of my dearest friends, Anna and John, went through a hostile divorce. It was John's sin that led to the dissolution of their marriage. They almost never see each other now. The rare occasions since their separation where they have been in the same room together are always (understandably) tense for everyone involved, but they are especially difficult for Anna.

When John was seriously injured in a car accident, my husband and I went to visit him in the hospital. The three of us spent the morning together before we had to leave to meet a friend for lunch. We told John that we would stop back by to check on him later and asked if he wanted anything from the restaurant. He said he'd love a chocolate peanut butter milkshake. What we didn't mention to John was that we were going out to eat with Anna.

Over lunch, Anna asked about John's health, and we prayed for him when we said grace. As we were finishing the meal, I asked our waiter to add John's milkshake to my tab. Anna said, "I'm paying for it. Put that milkshake on my bill." Then she leaned over to me and said, "Don't tell John it's from me." Before I could agree to this, she reconsidered and said, "I changed my mind. Tell him it's from me and that I am praying for his recovery." When Curtis and I walked back into John's hospital room and handed him the shake, I relayed the message from Anna. I will never forget the look of glad surprise on his face. He smiled and said softly, "Well, I'll be darned. Please make sure you tell her I say 'Thanks!'"

There's always some creative way that you can show grace to the people who have hurt you. Even in relationships that can't be reconciled fully, there are opportunities to show mercy, like Anna did. In marriages that are moving toward complete reconciliation, there will be many occasions for these loving interactions.

If your husband chooses repentance, it will bring honor to your Heavenly Father. Do you have a desire to warmly welcome your husband, even though his sin has brought you deep sorrow? Forgiving your husband might be the most difficult thing you ever do. It could also be one of the most significant ways you will ever display Christlike love.

Questions for Action, Discussion, and Reflection

1. What would it look like for you to address your husband's sin for his benefit?

2. If you've had self-righteous thoughts toward your husband, name them. How does this passage speak to them? Can you think of additional Bible verses that counter self-righteousness?

3. What does the parable of the unforgiving servant say about forgiveness (Matthew 18:21–35)?

4. Have you shown others the kind of forgiveness that makes your home a place where repentant sinners can flourish and grow?

5. Memorize John 15:5 and Colossians 3:13.

6. Today's passage contrasted two ways of interacting with repentant sinners. What would it look like for you to warmly welcome your husband if he puts off porn? Are you prepared to welcome him this way?

Further Reading on Forgiveness

Powlison, David. *Good and Angry: Redeeming Anger, Irritation, Complaining, and Bitterness*, chapter 7. Greensboro, NC: New Growth Press, 2016.

Satrom, Hayley. *Forgiveness: Reflecting God's Mercy.* 31-Day Devotionals for Life. Phillipsburg, NJ: P & R Publishing, 2020.

11

Growth through Suffering

ONE SUMMER MY family vacationed in the mountains of rural Georgia, a region known for its waterfalls. While there we visited a state park that features a rushing river with a natural rockslide that is situated between two sparkling pools which form perfect swimming holes.

On the morning we went, the sun-dappled cove was occupied by only one other family and several varieties of butterflies. Upon arrival, we took in the gorgeous scenery for a few minutes as the butterflies fluttered lazily along the water's edge and occasionally landed on our outstretched hands. Then we placed our belongings in the shade and slowly navigated the steep embankment that led to the upper pool. The water was clear and cold. It took my breath away. As I perched on the highest point preparing for my first slide, I ran my hands over the rocks. They were covered with a thin layer of slippery algae, which made gliding to the bottom swift and comfortable. I pushed off, slid down the falls, and landed laughing in the pool below. Looking back, that morning was a highlight of our trip.

Eventually, we began to shiver in the chilly water and returned to the bank for a picnic. The sun warmed us while we ate. Soon we were refreshed and ready for another round of sliding. We had just dipped back into the pool when three fishermen, grandfatherly in appearance, entered the cove. The parents of other small children were sunning on large, flat rocks beside the lower pool. From this vantage point, they were keeping watch over their kids. The fishermen climbed those same rocks and flanked the seated parents. Without saying a word, they began casting their lines (and hooks!) into the pool where the kids were floating on inflatable rafts. The situation was even more distressing because one of the fishermen wore a hat bearing the logo of his local church.

I approached the fishermen and asked them to move to another pool, pointing out that we were enjoying the cove first and that their hooks posed a safety risk to the children. I also reminded them that the river was full of similar waterfalls and fishing holes within a few minutes' walk of the rock slide, but this was the only slide. They continued to fish while I spoke and then staunchly refused to stop casting into the waters, replying that they had just as much right to be there as we did because their fishing licenses paid for the parks department to stock all the pools with fish. One of them even assured me that he had been fishing long enough to know how to avoid accidentally hooking a child. I quickly realized nothing could be said to convince them to move or wait their turn. Our picturesque day ended abruptly. We were unable to enjoy the pool safely. So both families had to pack up and leave the park.

As my family drove away, our sons grew increasingly frustrated. One of them commented that he absolutely couldn't believe the way those fishermen had treated us. My child's assessment of the situation was accurate. I also recognized in his bitter rehashing of the day's events an unholy tendency that I must resist within myself. It's not difficult to point out my suffering when I am the victim of someone else's sin. We were innocent bystanders at the rock slide. We were mistreated by those men. They were singularly focused on a selfish agenda. We suffered (a minor inconvenience in this example) because of their behavior. To make matters more frustrating, I still don't understand the rationale behind their insistence on fishing below the slide. Children had been swimming and splashing in that small pool all morning. Surely any fish would have vacated the area hours earlier to avoid the commotion. Their rude behavior was pointless. See what I mean? Airing a grievance comes naturally.

Building a Bridge of Grace

It's easier to give grace to people who struggle with the same kinds of sins that I do. When I don't think that I can relate to another person's struggles, bridging the gap to enter his or her world can feel impossible. You might be looking at your husband's porn use from this perspective. If pornography is not something that you find tempting, your husband might seem a lot like the fishermen on my vacation. Perhaps you are completely disgusted by the thought of looking at a stranger's body or watching people's most intimate moments. If so, on top of all the other significant emotions that accompany betrayal by a spouse, his sin has probably left you feeling bewildered.

The goals of this chapter are to begin building a bridge between your husband's struggles and your own and to encourage you to think of specific ways God might be using this suffering to make you more like Jesus. As you learn to relate to your spouse in his struggle, it will be easier to come alongside him and help him fight for purity. It will also be easier to see the refining work God is doing in your life through this adversity. Learning to look for and trust God's purposes for suffering will be one protection from bitterness. Steve Viars puts it this way: "Every moment spent trusting God and following his commands is a moment that is not invested in brewing more bitterness."[1]

As you seek to understand your husband's struggle with pornography, it will be helpful to keep your own struggles in mind, especially if you find his actions incomprehensible. After all, he has risked injury to your marriage for the fleeting lure of sexual images. This is a terrible exchange! When initially assessing the situation, some spouses don't think they can relate. I sure didn't! To come alongside those who struggle with issues that you do not find tempting, it is helpful to look deeper than the outward behavior and try to understand the reason he keeps returning to this sin. If your husband reads this book's companion, *Redeem Your Marriage: Hope for Husbands Who Have Hurt through Pornography* by Curtis Solomon, he will be encouraged to think through his specific triggers so that he can better fight temptation. Although motivations and manifestations vary from person to person, the bedrock of lustful actions is familiar to everyone.

A person who lusts gives in to an overgrown desire. Lusting after something means wanting it too much. (For example, fishing isn't wrong, but a lust for fishing can result in risking harm to small children just to seize an opportunity to cast into a favorite fishing hole.) If you've ever sinned to satisfy any disproportionate desire, then to a certain extent you can relate to sexual lust. You can also surely relate to some of the other actions and attitudes that precede and follow porn use. There's usually lying involved. Have you ever lied to get what you want or to keep other people happy? Lack of self-control is common too. Can you think of any areas where you lack self-control? Pride and unbelief are two more reasons people think they can get away with viewing porn. Do you ever think you know your needs better than God does? Do you ever live life as though you aren't dependent on God? He always sees, knows, and cares what you are doing. During a typical day, do you remember that he is present and upholding you?

Practicing the Presence of God

God's always right there with us, but we forget him so easily. That's true of people watching porn, just as it's true of the rest of us when we give in to other temptations. I recently revisited an enduring book called *The Practice of the Presence of God*. It's a compilation of letters written in the 1600s by Brother Lawrence. He lived at a monastery in Paris and worked as a cook. His foremost desire in life was "to walk as in (God's) presence" every single moment.[2] For almost 400 years, Christians before us have recognized the virtue of Brother Lawrence's aim to acknowledge reality by treating God as though he is ever present. Brother Lawrence describes one aspect of his communion with God this way: "As for my set hours of prayer, they are only a continuation of the same exercise. Sometimes I consider myself there as a stone before a carver, whereof he is to make a statue; presenting myself thus before God, I desire Him to form His perfect image in my soul, and make me entirely like Himself."[3]

When you pray, are you constantly speaking to God? Do you ever take time to sit quietly in his presence? Do you pause to imagine the work that he could be doing in your soul? How is he carving you right now? What circumstances form the tools he is using to smooth out existing roughness and make Jesus more visible in your life? Have you considered that God is so loving and powerful that he has plans to use your husband's worst sins and the hardest moments of your marriage to do a beautifying, refining work in your life?

That day at the rock slide my family experienced the consequences of someone else's overgrown desire. As we drove away, we talked with our kids about the experience.

"How does it make you feel that those men decided to fish in the pool where you were swimming?" I asked.

"I feel sad, frustrated, and angry," said one of my sons.

"That's how I feel too. Sometimes I am really, really selfish. Have you ever seen me act selfishly?"

"Yes!"

"Have you ever been selfish?"

"Yes."

130

"How do you think your selfish behavior made other people feel?"

"They probably felt pretty bad."

"Sometimes I act just like those fishermen. There are days I am so focused on pursuing what I want that I spoil the day for you guys and for Dad. Recognizing other people's sin is much easier than recognizing my own. Let's try to remember how we feel right now. The next time I am tempted to sin I want to remember that if I choose to commit that sin other people will be hurt by my actions. I don't want to be the source of another person's pain. I want to please God by counting other people as better than myself (Philippians 2:3)."

Moving from Bitterness to Humility

When your husband's sin impacts you, you could choose to remain focused on his sin. This type of reflection is likely to result in bitterness. Conversely, you could use the suffering to build sensitivity toward the ways your actions impact others. Being mistreated hurts. When I mistreat other people, I hurt them, too. Let's ask God to help us remember how terrible it feels when we get the brunt of sinful behavior. Let's also ask him to help us learn to love others more than we love ourselves. Spotting a glaring transgression in another person or suffering because of another person's sinful decision is an opportunity to look for similar tendencies within myself. This type of introspection leads away from bitterness and towards humility.

What if being sinned against gives you pause to consider the type of person you could become in Christ? What if being subject to another person's sin leads to detesting and forsaking your own sin? Would the suffering be worth the growth?

Questions for Action, Discussion, and Reflection

1. As you've reflected on this chapter, has God revealed ways that you and your husband's sin struggles are more similar than you previously knew?

2. Take some time to contemplate how God might be chipping away the sin in your life through all the difficult experiences that lead you to read this book. How is he currently making you more like himself?

3. Are you able to honestly say that the suffering has been worth the growth?

4. Has resentment toward your husband built up in your heart? Meditate on Ephesians 4:31–32. What is the reason Paul gives for being kind, compassionate, and forgiving toward others?

5. Pray daily that God will enable you and your husband to grow more aware of God's constant loving presence.

Further Reading on Living Continually in God's Presence

Brother Lawrence. *The Practice of the Presence of God.* Westwood, NJ: Fleming H. Revell Company, 1958.

Further Reading on Bitterness

Viars, Steve. *Overcoming Bitterness: Moving from Life's Greatest Hurts to a Life Filled with Joy.* Grand Rapids: Baker Books, a division of Baker Publishing Group, 2021.

Further Reading on Suffering

Powlison, David. *God's Grace in Your Suffering,* Wheaton, IL: 2018.

12

Not Another Hallmark Movie

ABIGAIL SUCCEEDED. BY God's grace, she staved off David's attack and returned home. When she arrived, Nabal was full from his feast and very drunk. She wisely let him sleep it off, waiting until the next morning to recount news of her campaign on his behalf (1 Samuel 25:36). Here's what happened next: "In the morning, when the wine had gone out of Nabal, his wife told him these things, and his heart died within him, and he became as a stone. And about ten days later the Lord struck Nabal, and he died" (1 Samuel 25:37–38).

When David found out about Nabal's death, he asked Abigail to become his wife. She accepted. The first time I read this story I was a teenager and didn't have the biblical literacy to accurately place Abigail in the timeline of David's life. So I imagined this happy wedding as the story's ending. Taken out of its broader context, 1 Samuel 25 is reminiscent of the plots of several 1990s animated films: Beautiful, smart, rich lady subverts a curmudgeon and does something very, *very* brave. Her actions save the day. The bad guy croaks. Then the scruffy, hot guy (with the most beautiful eyes) turns out to be the next king. He proposes! She accepts! They marry! I distinctly remember the relief I felt when Abigail was rescued from the clutches of obtuse Nabal and quickly received a proposal from David, thereby getting her very own Happily Ever After! But my assumptions were naive (and historically inaccurate). This kingly David, a seeming "total package" (poet-warrior, man after God's own heart), was a complicated person.

I know now what I didn't know then—Abigail didn't get a perfect marriage the second time around. As we mature in Christ, it becomes easier to accept the tension that we are all convoluted—including David. Your husband is more than his porn problem. If that's your primary focus, you could mistakenly appraise him as solely a project to be fixed rather than a person who, along with his sin struggles, also has admirable attributes. It may be tempting to daydream about the what-ifs of life spent with your college ex-boyfriend who didn't work out, but (way back then) loved Jesus so much more than your apathetic spouse does today. Perhaps time and distance have polished all memories so that some other guy glows as a shining example of manhood. Those daydreams are mirages—just like porn. Your spouse shouldn't have to compete with a fantasy Prince Charming. Because of the covenant vows you made, your actual husband deserves your focused love and affection just as much as you deserve his. Take time each day to thank your husband for the ways he loves and serves your family. In all circumstances there are reasons to be grateful. If you can't think of any, pray that God will reveal some. Ask the Lord to give you a gracious attitude toward your husband. Then entrust yourself to Christ, even as you are experiencing heartache.

Second only to Jesus, Curtis is the best gift God has ever given me. I am writing this chapter in the fall. Right now, our yard is littered with leaves. From the desk where I am writing in my second-floor office, I can see Curtis outside raking. It's a tiring job and there are lots of other things he would rather do with his time, but he wants our yard to be beautiful. It's not just our yard that he's learning to tend well. He is also cooperating with God's spirit by working hard at tending the fallen leaves in his life. With God's help, I am cooperating as well—it takes three people to make a marriage flourish. Curtis is not perfect, and we don't have a perfect marriage. But he's the perfect husband for me.

As I reflect on the imperfect beauty of my own marriage, I am reminded of the many reasons that I dislike the way romance is depicted in Hallmark Movies, romance novels (including most Christian romance novels), and the plots of 1990s princess cartoons. The two problems with romance stories most relevant to our discussion include the way they oversimplify the complexities of relationships by neatly resolving trials in ways that don't match reality and the way they foster discontent by setting up impossible standards. When people encounter realistic depictions of love, they should come away better equipped to express love and accomplish good deeds. A love story that is true and beautiful will help fan into flame hope and gratitude. Try to recall the last time you consumed media from the romance genre. Did you come away thanking God for your husband, desiring to love and serve him more, or did you feel more frustrated with him, more tempted to fantasize about the life you'd rather have, and more likely to scrutinize his flaws? This should serve as a litmus test for whether the romance stories you consume are beneficial or harmful to your soul and your marriage.

As I considered how to end this book, I found myself initially falling into the rom-com trap. I was looking for a way to wrap things up neatly—until I realized that being honest with you is more loving than putting a pretty bow on this story. There's not a Hallmark version of the Christian pilgrimage toward heaven. If I tried to give you fairy-tale assurances, my words would be empty and useless to you, or worse still, they might form unrealistic expectations that are bound to disappoint you. The truth is that I don't know how your marriage is going to turn out, and I don't know how mine is going to turn out either. I hope that your next chapter contains repentance, restoration, and unity, but that chapter hasn't been written yet. Each of us is living a story in the making.

The final destination is heaven for every person who loves Jesus, but if you've been a Christian for any length of time, you already know that. It's not a coincidence that Scripture refers to Jesus as the bridegroom and the church as his bride (2 Corinthians 11:2). All marriages are fractured, foggy representations of the relationship between Jesus and the church. Your desires for love, acceptance, a resolute pursuer, and faithfulness are good desires! However, if you think your husband will ever be able to do any of those things perfectly, you are looking to the wrong man. You can't demand perfection from him; that's impossible. No one has ever experienced a perfect marriage here on earth. They don't exist. Your husband cannot be your Savior.

Jesus tells us that in heaven, we won't be married or given in marriage (Luke 20:34–35). If you are inquisitive like me, you probably have lots of questions about what that means. Sorry, I don't have many answers for you. But I can tell you that the assurance from Jesus that we won't miss what is such a central relationship here on earth gives us a glimpse into how satisfying it will be to live united with the church in the presence of God. We will experience love so bountiful and consuming that all the tears we've cried over our marriages will be dried and all the joys of being a wife will be eclipsed by union with Christ. Everything you ever hoped your marriage would be will pale in comparison to spending eternity with Jesus!

Let Your Faith Interpret Life's Hardships

You haven't missed your happily ever after. Realizing that it still lies ahead will help you to shake off fantasy and focus on entering fully into the realities of your own story. Today we are going to explore another chapter in Abigail's life. I've heard others say that the first year of marriage is the hardest. That's not always the case, but the first few years of Abigail and David's marriage was certainly full of trials. At the time they wed, David was still evading Saul, who was trying to kill him. I don't know about you, but I have never lived under the threat of a murderous king (who has an entire army at his command). Abigail is once again a bride. But now she's married to a man who is on the run.

Contrast her new life with the one she left behind. She came to her second marriage accustomed to the comfort that wealth provides.[1] Five maids attended her as she traveled to wed David. This detail clues us in to the extent of her wealth. Five is "more than any other Israelite woman in the Bible is said to have had."[2] Although it was surely shocking to adapt to David's lifestyle, there's evidence that Abigail joyfully accepted the discomforts of newlywed life alongside a man who spent his days hiding in caves and evading assassination attempts. Do you remember when Nabal took the dynamics between David and Saul at face value? He viewed David as King Saul's disobedient servant (1 Samuel 25:10). Even before Nabal's death, Abigail refused to align herself with his faithless assessment. She chose to evaluate circumstances in a way that prioritized God's appraisal of the situation. She affirmed David's "lasting dynasty" before it came to pass (1 Samuel 25:28, 30 NIV). This gives us good reason to believe that when Abigail came up against dismal circumstances in her first few years with David, she continued through them with unwavering faith.

Faith interprets the hardships of life with an ongoing, focused belief that God's promises are coming true even though good outcomes are not yet in view. How do you talk to yourself and to others about your marital strain? Even while lamenting the pain and difficulty, you can also speak of the lasting dynasty you will inherit through Jesus.

Abigail's faith prepared her for the difficulties of marriage, as did her humility. When David's servants arrived to usher Abigail to the wedding ceremony, she said to them, "Behold, your handmaid is a servant to wash the feet of the servants of my lord" (1 Samuel 25:41). The depth of her humility throughout this chapter reminds me of 1 Peter 3:4: "Let your adorning be the hidden person of the heart with the imperishable beauty of a gentle and quiet spirit, which in God's sight is very precious." The words Peter uses here point wives to Jesus. One of the reasons a gentle spirit is so precious to God is that this attitude imitates the character of his son Jesus, who describes himself as gentle (Matthew 11:29). Wives can follow Christ's example when facing the uncertain, unwritten chapters of marriage (1 Peter 2:23). Think about some of the ways you can show your husband Christlike gentleness as you read the following description:

> The Greek word translated "gentle" here occurs just three other times in the New Testament: in the first beatitude, that "the *meek*" will inherit the earth (Matt. 5:5); in the prophecy in Matthew 21:5 (quoting Zechariah 9:9) that Jesus the king "is coming to you, *humble*, and mounted on a donkey"; and in Peter's encouragement to wives to nurture more than anything else "the hidden person of the heart with the imperishable beauty of a *gentle* and quiet spirit" (1 Pet. 3:4). Meek. Humble. Gentle. Jesus is not trigger-happy. Not harsh, reactionary, easily exasperated. He is the most understanding person in the universe. The posture most natural to him is not a pointed finger but open arms.[3]

Abigail exemplifies faith and gentleness, and these surely carried her through intense physical and relational pressures. In addition to the hardship of wondering if her new husband would be captured by Saul, I wonder how Abigail reckoned with the reality that she didn't have David's exclusive love and devotion. Around the same time that she married him, he took another wife named Ahinoam. Later he added additional wives and concubines to the family (1 Samuel 25:43; 1 Chronicles 3:1–9).

Scripture never comments on whether Nabal committed sexual sins, but it does detail David's polygamy and his sexual predation of Bathsheba (along with his murderous scheme against her husband). He made these decisions after his marriage to Abigail. In some respects, Abigail traded in one set of hardships for another.

Although the end of chapter 25 wraps up neatly, like a Hallmark movie, the reader quickly realizes that the honeymoon phase is brief (perhaps even nonexistent). Chapter 27 describes how David (along with his wives, 600 soldiers, and their families) fled to an area called Gath, which, at that time, was under the control of the Philistines. Achish, the King of Gath, mistakenly thought that David was fighting against Israel, so he trusted David and gave him a town called Ziklag (1 Samuel 27:6). David and all who fled with him inhabited that town for one year and four months.

Abigail's decision to entwine her own story with David's brought her highs, lows, and plot twists that otherwise would not have occurred. But I suspect that when I ask her in heaven, she will point to those moments of fear and uncertainty as sacred events in which God showed his care for her in powerful ways, thus helping her learn to lean more heavily on him. Learning to trust God was a far better gift than anything she might have gained had her marriages been smooth sailing. The next major episode in Abigail's life was recorded in 1 Samuel 30, and after this story we don't learn many more details about her. It's noted that she gives birth to David's second son (2 Samuel 3:3), Chileab (he's also called Daniel in 1 Chronicles 3:1). Other than this birth announcement, 1 Samuel 30 is the last of Abigail's adventures recorded in the Bible. This passage is also where we will spend the remainder of our time together.

Allow me to set the scene for you: Abigail had been living in Ziklag for over a year (1 Samuel 27:3). Throughout this time, David continued to obey God's word by conquering the promised land.[4] All along David kept his military campaigns hidden from Achish and remained in his favor (1 Samuel 27:12).

At the beginning of 1 Samuel 28, the Philistines gathered to fight against Israel (the troops that Saul commanded). King Saul saw the gathered enemy, and he was afraid. He sought God, but God didn't answer. Next Saul decided to consult a medium, even though Scripture absolutely forbids this pagan practice. His disobedient actions were met with a swift resolution: "This section presents . . . perhaps the darkest moment in Saul's life, his deliberate violation of one of the most serious prohibitions in the Torah (cf. 1 Chr 10:13–14). By turning to a medium to receive guidance for his life, Saul committed a capital offense (cf. Lev 20:6). Less than twenty-four hours after he did so, he was dead."[5]

Now we come to the story of David's activities, which overlap with the events immediately preceding Saul's death. I want to leave you with this account because it demonstrates how to faithfully navigate whatever hardships might appear between yourself and heaven. While Saul disregarded God in preparation for his final, tragic battle against the Philistines, David's army drew near their home in Ziklag. During the previous three days, they had marched about 75 miles.[6] They finally arrived in Ziklag, exhausted and anticipating a warm welcome, supper, and comfortable beds. Instead, they were greeted by devastation.

> Now when David and his men came to Ziklag on the third day, the Amalekites had made a raid against the Negeb and against Ziklag. They had overcome Ziklag and burned it with fire and taken captive the women and all who were in it, both small and great. They killed no one, but carried them off and went their way. And when David and his men came to the city, they found it burned with fire, and their wives and sons and daughters taken captive. Then David and the people who were with him raised their voices and wept until they had no

more strength to weep. David's two wives also had been taken captive, Ahinoam of Jezreel and Abigail the widow of Nabal of Carmel. (1 Samuel 30:1–5)

Earlier in 1 Samuel, God instructed Saul to completely destroy the Amalekites. Saul chose to disobey. He left some of them alive. As a result, God rejected him as king (1 Samuel 15:17–33). His disobedience led to these smoldering ruins in Ziklag. To put it another way, Abigail's captivity was a direct result of Saul's sin.[7] As you face any difficulties brought on by your husband's disobedience, remember the hopeful flip side of this idea. You already know that it's possible to face hardships that are the direct result of someone else's sin. But, if that's true, then it's also possible to encounter blessings that result from someone else's obedience to God. Pray that you will be faithful to do the things that God has brought to mind as you've read this book. Pray that your obedience now will lead to concrete blessings for others in the years to come.

Earlier we thought through the practice of lament. This story from David's life narrates that spiritual discipline. Here David called out to God in his distress. Each of the psalms of lament he composed came as a result of real-life sorrow. How does knowing that impact the way you read these words that David wrote? "I am lonely and afflicted. The troubles of my heart are enlarged; bring me out of my distresses" (Psalm 25:16–17).[8]

Lament turned David's heart toward God, but it didn't cause his difficulties to stop. This dire situation was about to get even worse. Lament prepared David to seek God's help again when his closest companions turned on him. Look at the way David's troops responded to the scorched remains of their home:

And David was greatly distressed, for the people spoke of stoning him, because all the people were bitter in soul, each for his sons and daughters. But David strengthened himself in the LORD his God. And David said to Abiathar the priest, the son of Ahimelech, "Bring me the ephod." So Abiathar brought the ephod to David. And David inquired of the LORD, "Shall I pursue after this band? Shall I overtake them?" He answered him, "Pursue, for you shall surely overtake and shall surely rescue." So David set out, and the six hundred men who were with him . . . . (1 Samuel 30:6–9a)

Although this dilemma was not David's fault, his troops momentarily turned their hearts against him and considered stoning him. David wasn't an unflappable stoic. He was rightly distressed by these awful circumstances. The stakes were huge. His family and friends were in danger. People under his care needed rescue. David went straight to the only one who could provide what he needed, which was strength and a wise strategy to face another difficult military campaign. At the same time that David ran to God, Saul defied God and ran to a medium, determined to fix the problem in his own way (1 Samuel 28:7–19).[9] Two men prepared to face powerful enemies. Both were at the end of their own strength. Both were unsure of how to proceed. Only one of them honored God. David didn't shy away from God. He obeyed God's law, turning quickly to God to ask for direction and help and following the clear commands laid out in Scripture.

The way we interpret hard times in life determines whether we go to God or rely on some other source for strength. David and Saul's example shows us that trusting God makes all the difference:

> David's genius was his spiritual resilience. He expected to find the resources he needed in the Lord his God, and he was not disappointed, whereas Saul had made a habit of "doing his own thing," and deliberately refusing to carry out the instructions he was given by Samuel. David

refused to interpret obstacles as signs of opposition to him; rather they provided opportunities to see what [God] would do in answer to the prayer of his servant.[10]

We are not given insight into how Abigail handled her brief time of captivity, but we can reasonably speculate, based on the way she handled past difficulties, that she responded to this latest trial similarly to David—by trusting in the Lord and acting in faith and obedience. How do you interact with troubles in your life? Do you rely on God and seek his wisdom when disaster strikes? Do you continue to obey God when life is difficult? Do you ever justify acts of disobedience when circumstances seem unfair? Do you interpret mounting problems as evidence that God is working against you, or do you see your troubles as an opportunity for God to work for you?[11]

Strengthen Yourself in the Lord

I can't guarantee that your husband will never again give in to the temptation to view porn. In view of that truth, these are the questions you need to answer: What will I do if my husband returns to pornography? How can I get through the pain faithfully? The answer is found in David's example. First, turn toward God in lament. Second, resolve to obey God during the trouble. Third, trust that God is not opposing you, and believe that this is an opportunity for God to work for your good, even if circumstances continue to worsen. Next, *strengthen yourself in the Lord*. This means asking God to give you comfort and energy to face this current trial. Finally, seek God's wisdom and seek the guidance of your local church family by asking wise friends for counsel and asking God to show you the next step to take.[12] If God has already shown you what to do next, then take that step by faith. As you do, remember the central theme of 1 Samuel: God is always with you, and he will fight your battles!

Questions for Action, Discussion, and Reflection

1. Have you been tempted to escape into a fantasy world to alleviate the pressure of your difficult marriage? If yes, explain this struggle.

2. What will you do if your husband returns to pornography?

3. Remember and discuss a time that you strengthened your-self in the Lord.

4. What is the central theme of 1 Samuel? How have you seen this theme play out in your life?

Further Reading on God's Extravagant Love

Ortlund, Dane. *Gentle and Lowly: The Heart of Christ for Sinners and Sufferers.* Wheaton, IL: Crossway, 2020.

Appendix 1

Porn and Abuse

MY GREATEST DESIRE in writing this book is to glorify God by helping hurting women. As I prayed and wrote, wrote and prayed, God laid on my heart the need to care for a special group of women in a way that would meet them in their particular needs. Those women are valued daughters of God who find themselves in an abusive relationship. While much of the truth I offer in the book is still applicable to them, the dynamics of abuse would make some of the advice more harmful than helpful. I am not an expert in abuse care, so I reached out to a number of people who have a great deal of knowledge and experience in caring for people who have been abused.[1] I've compiled their responses to my questions in the following appendix. I pray that it is helpful and brings some clarity to a dark and difficult situation.

Throughout the interviews and addressing multiple questions, the advice that came up most often was the need for you to talk to someone about your situation. You need a "trustworthy person" or "trustworthy friend" who encapsulates the following characteristics:

1. She is a mature Christian.
2. She understands the dynamics of abuse. She has categories for understanding what abuse is, the various ways

it plays out in relationships, and how to walk through this difficulty with you. It is ideal to find someone who already has experience walking with others through abuse situations.

3. She is committed to your safety and to moving at your speed. She is not going to rush you into anything, and she is looking out for your best interests.

4. She is committed to walking alongside you through the process.

I encourage you to find a trustworthy friend sooner rather than later. The sooner you get help, the better. You have been trying to deal with this on your own for too long already. God does not intend for you to bear this burden alone; please accept his help through his people.

The remainder of this appendix is formatted around a number of questions I posed to the panel of experts. I've rephrased the questions into statements so that it reads as encouragement for you rather than questions to be answered.

1. If you already know you are in an abusive relationship and you came to this appendix for help, the most important things for you to know are . . .

First, remember that God loves you. He hates what you are facing and desires change for you and your husband. He has also provided help for you in loving Christians who are familiar with situations like yours and who want to help.

Secondly, know that you do not need to face this alone. No one is meant to walk through any trial alone. The more serious the trial, the more we need the help of others. We encourage you to find a trustworthy person who is experienced in caring for people in abusive relationships. Find someone who understands what abuse is, the many ways in which it manifests in a relationship, and how to deal with it. Hopefully you are in a church with these trustworthy people. If your church has a ministry that cares for people in hard situations, you may find a trustworthy person to talk to there. If not, look for a counselor at www.calledtopeace .org, or https://fieldstonecounseling.org/services.

Thirdly, it is important to know that none of your husband's sin is your fault. Even when Eve enticed Adam to sin, God did not hold Eve responsible for his sin. God held Adam responsible for his actions (Genesis 3). No matter what you have done or not done, your husband's sin is his responsibility. You did not bring his sin upon yourself.

A fourth important thing to keep in mind is that your husband's pornography use is not the most important issue at hand. We recognize that you came to this book because of your husband's battle with pornography, but it is important to know that the most important thing that needs to be dealt with is his heart that is bent toward both abuse and pornography. While they are distinct behaviors, there is a great deal of overlap in the heart behind abuse and pornography use. They both have a warped view of the world that sees others as a means to an end. People become objects to be used, not persons to be loved. Your husband's struggle with pornography is serious, but his abuse is a far greater concern and should be the focus of attention in this season of life.

A fifth thing to consider is developing a safety plan for yourself and anyone else in your home that is being abused. Again, it would be best to develop the plan with a trustworthy friend who understands your situation and is walking with you through it. You can get a template to help you develop a safety plan that is tailored to yours and your family's needs in appendix A of *Is it Abuse?* by Darby Strickland (P & R, 2020), or visit one of these websites: www.thehotline.org/plan-for-safety/, http://bradhambrick .com/safetyplan/.

2. If you are reading this appendix because you are not sure whether or not you are being abused, here are some things to consider:

If the thought that you might be in an abusive relationship even comes to mind, you are suffering. You are facing a difficult, challenging, hurtful situation. I echo the message above—you are not meant to walk this hard road alone. The best thing you can do is begin to investigate your relationship with someone outside it. Again, I recommend that you find someone who understands abuse and how it plays out in marriage. I encourage you to check with your church first and then with the sources we mentioned above.

Here are some behaviors that often take place in an abusive relationship. As you read these questions, preferably with a trustworthy friend, consider whether or not they occur in your relationship:[2]

Does your partner . . .

☐ Embarrass or humiliate you in front of others?
☐ Push, grab, or shove you?
☐ Lie to you regularly?
☐ Make you feel like you're walking on eggshells?
☐ Often seem angry at someone or something?
☐ Deprive you of sleep?
☐ Tell you how to dress or act?
☐ Pressure you for sex in ways that make you feel uncomfortable?
☐ Make you feel crazy?
☐ Use weapons to scare you?
☐ Ignore you or give you the silent treatment?
☐ Blame you for how he treats you or for anything bad that happens?
☐ Check up on you excessively?
☐ Use the children to control you? Try to turn the children against you?

❐ Make all the decisions about money?

❐ Try to isolate you by controlling where you go, who you see, and what you do?

❐ Intimidate you with looks, gestures, cursing, or a loud voice?

❐ Degrade you, make you feel insignificant, powerless, and/or worthless?

❐ Slap, pinch, push, or kick you?

❐ Choke you?

❐ Minimize or deny his abusive behavior?

❐ Threaten to hurt or punish you if you don't do what he wants?

❐ Threaten to leave you, hurt you, or commit suicide?

❐ Act extremely jealous?

❐ Often criticize you, your friends, or your family?

❐ Destroy your property, possessions, or documents?

If any of these behaviors are present, please reach out and find a trustworthy person to talk to immediately.

3. In chapters 6 and 7, I encouraged you to confront your husband's sin. However, if you are, or suspect you may be, in an abusive relationship that advice would not be appropriate for you. Here are some things to consider that are different for your situation than for the wife who is not in an abusive relationship.

If you already know you are in an abusive relationship, you were probably scared even at the thought of confronting your husband over his pornography use. You are totally justified in that fear. It would be terrifying and potentially dangerous for you to do so. Our advice for you is *not* to confront your husband's pornography use. Instead, consider the advice above to get help as you walk through your experience of abuse.

If you aren't sure, but you think you might be in an abusive relationship, the fear you have over this question may give some insight into your situation. No one feels good about confronting the sin of another person, but victims of abuse will have well-grounded terror at the very idea. If you are fairly confident that your confrontation would result in some kind of punishment or consequence, then you have more reason to suspect you are in an abusive relationship. Review the questions above, if you haven't already, to get further insight into your relationship. And of course, share your thoughts with a trustworthy person.

4. In chapter 10, I encourage women to warmly welcome repentant husbands. However, that advice should be different if a woman has been or is being abused by her husband. Some differences include how to identify repentance from abuse and pornography use.

First, it is important to emphasize that in these situations we are looking for repentance in both areas—abuse and pornography use, with a priority on the abuse.

Second, repentance in these areas, but especially in abuse, is very difficult to identify. Abusers are master liars and manipulators. They can say all the right things and check off boxes and to-dos very well. They may even look really "repentant" with weeping and seemingly broken hearts. However, they are often manifesting what the Bible calls "worldly sorrow," not genuine "godly sorrow" (2 Corinthians 7:9-11 NIV). Both may have similar outward manifestations in the beginning: crying, promises of change, etc. However, godly sorrow is demonstrated over the long term by genuine repentance. Worldly sorrow doesn't lead to true change, but actually leads to death (2 Corinthians 7:10).

"Whoever hates disguises himself with his lips and harbors deceit in his heart; when he speaks graciously, believe him not, for there are seven abominations in his heart; though his hatred be covered with deception, his wickedness will be exposed in the assembly" (Proverbs 26:24–26). These verses highlight the deceptive capabilities of haters. It is in their nature to lie and deceive, and that requires (others) "the assembly," (and time) "will be exposed" to discern genuine repentance.

True repentance bears fruit (Matthew 3:8; Luke 3:8; Acts 26:20). Repentance is a transformation in one's heart. The fruit is a transformation in living. Fruit manifests over time in a changed lifestyle.

This book has argued for the involvement of other people in the process of repentance and restoration from pornography use. In cases of abuse this is a must. Everyone who works in the abuse/domestic violence field recommends a team approach to these situations. It will be important for the team to be involved in investigating and assessing genuine repentance. This is not left up to you to determine on your own. The team should develop a plan that includes specific manifestations of repentance that need to be present for some time. Darby Strickland offers some excellent advice for assessing genuine repentance in her article, "How to Discern True Repentance When Serious Sin Has Occurred."[3]

Your care team needs to determine the steps of restoration, when and how you will go back with your spouse. The care team also needs to maintain some level of contact with you and your spouse to ensure that repentance continues. The consequences of "quick forgiveness" in pornography can be devastating to a marriage. The consequences in cases of abuse can be deadly.

A word of warning and encouragement to you as a wife: as you step forward with others to get help for you and your family, it is going to be very hard. There will likely be a recommended season of separation from your husband. This is a trial in and of itself. You will be tempted to rush back in because you miss your husband, you don't like being separated, you want the father of your children in their lives, etc. All of these desires are good, but you need to prioritize God's glory and the safety of your family above having those desires met. It will be difficult, but hang in there. Persevere for something better. Rushing back to your husband before he is genuinely repentant will thwart the efforts of God and your care team and likely escalate his sin. Trust the people and the process that God has brought around you. Let them make hard decisions, and follow their lead.

5. If you are reading this book alongside a friend and suspect or discover in the process that your friend is being abused, here are some concepts to help you.

Assuming you are not an expert in this field, one of the first things you need to do is get more information. You are not *the* solution to your friend's problem, but if you learn and address it well you can become *part* of the solution. You will find resources under statement 6 that can help you to learn more.

It is of utmost importance that you stay calm and don't rush yourself or your friend. You should not be the one to report the abuse or make the abuse public knowledge. This may sound contradictory to everything in your soul, and you might be confused by ideas like "mandatory reporting." In most jurisdictions, domestic violence, or intimate partner violence as it is often called now, is not a mandatory reporting situation (while violence against children and the elderly typically are). Without the ability to give you all the reasons, the primary thing you need to understand is that going public or reporting the abuse will put your friend in more danger. Her safety is your priority, and running to the authorities or rushing her to report will decrease her safety.

Multiple people we interviewed discouraged using the term *abuse*, unless your friend has told you that she is being abused. Many victims of abuse don't understand their situation as abuse. Most don't want to use or think in those terms. Many want to defend their husbands and will likely shut down if they hear that terminology. Even if your friend has revealed to you one story of abuse, your overreaction would likely shut her down. If you react in a shocked way, get enraged, and push her to report, she will likely not open up further.

If she has not told you she is being abused or told you any stories of abuse but you suspect it, you can begin to help by listening well, as well as becoming more educated in this area. This will involve asking good questions, listening, being patient, and praying.

Then you can start to explore by expressing concern: "I've seen some things in your marriage that concern me." Tell her some of the things you've observed and ask her what she thinks about those experiences. Some phrases that might indicate the control that often comes with abuse are "he won't let me," "he's making me do . . . ," "I provoke him," "I need to be careful about how I say . . . ," and "Please don't tell anyone." If you hear these things, ask for more information. Do so gently, kindly, not pushing, but caring.

If she tells you one story of abuse, she likely has hundreds if not thousands of other stories. Gently express sorrow, care, and concern. Let her know you are there for her. Ask her if there are other stories like that one, and listen to what she has to share. As more things come out, you will need to resist the growing temptation to rush, rage, and overreact. Pray with her and begin to give her words to express what she has faced.

If she opens up to you and is able to accept categories of abuse and affirm them in relation to her marriage, you can encourage her to seek more help with you. If your church has a care ministry that is equipped to walk through abuse, this is a great place to start. If not, you can find help at some of the ministries listed above and below.

6. The following are resources for more information on abuse/domestic violence:

Books

- Forrest, Joy. *Called to Peace: A Survivor's Guide to Finding Peace and Healing After Domestic Abuse.* Raleigh, NC: Blue Ink Press, 2018.
- Hambrick, Brad (ed.). *Becoming a Church that Cares Well for the Abused.* Nashville, TN: B & H Books, 2019.

- Holcomb, Justin and Lindsey. *Is It My Fault?: Hope and Healing for Those Suffering Domestic Violence.* Chicago, IL: Moody Publishers, 2014.
- Lawrence, Bernie and Ann Maree Goudzwaard. *Help[H]er: A Churchwide Response for Women in Crisis.* Lawrenceville, GA: PCA Committee on Discipleship Ministries, 2020.
- Moles, Chris. *The Heart of Domestic Abuse: Gospel Solutions for Men Who Use Control and Violence in the Home.* Bemidji, MN: Focus Publishing, 2015.
- Nicewater, Sue, and Maria Brookins. *Treasure in the Ashes: Our Journey Home from the Ruins of Sexual Abuse.* Wapwallopen, PA: Shepherd Press, 2018.
- Pierre, Jeremy, and Greg Wilson. *When Home Hurts: A Guide for Responding Wisely to Domestic Abuse in Your Church.* Scotland, UK: Christian Focus, 2021.
- Strickland, Darby. "Domestic Abuse: Help for the Sufferer." Resources for Changing Lives. Phillipsburg, NJ: P & R Publishing, 2018.
- Strickland, Darby. "Domestic Abuse: Recognize, Respond, Rescue." Resources for Changing Lives. Phillipsburg, NJ: P & R Publishing, 2018.
- Strickland, Darby. *Is it Abuse? A Biblical Guide to Identifying Domestic Abuse and Helping Victims.* Phillipsburg, NJ: P & R Publishing. (This book may be intimidating or too much for the victim of abuse, but it is an excellent resource for caregivers and friends.)

Organizations with multiple resources that you can access by searching "abuse"

Association of Biblical Counselors, https://christiancounseling.com
Biblical Counseling Coalition, https://www.biblicalcounselingcoalition.org/

Christian Counseling and Educational Foundation,
https://www.ccef.org/

National Domestic Abuse Hotline:
https://www.thehotline.org/, 800.799.SAFE

Training Opportunities

- Counseling Care for Domestic Abuse at https://ibcd.org/ (video training for counseling on domestic abuse, including role-playing counseling sessions).
- PeaceWorks University at https://www.chrismoles.org/

Websites

Becoming a Church That Cares Well for the Abused
https://churchcares.com/

Called to Peace Ministries https://www.calledtopeace.org/

Chris Moles (PeaceWorks) https://www.chrismoles.org/

Darby Strickland https://www.darbystrickland.com/

Help[H]er https://www.helpherresources.com/

When Home Hurts https://whenhomehurts.com/

7. This book is primarily written for wives who have been hurt by pornography in marriages where there is not abuse. However, porn use is often present in abusive relationships as well. Some considerations follow to help identify pornography use as abusive in and of itself or an accompaniment to additional forms of abuse.

There is a great deal of overlap between pornography use and abuse. Perpetrators of both objectify people. They see other humans not as humans, but as objects, tools, containers, and means to their own ends. The line between porn use of an abuser and that of a non-abuser is vague, and we won't try to make a clear line where one doesn't exist. Readers should be encouraged to investigate for abuse if they uncover pornography use and vice versa. Not because they always go hand in hand, but they can, and a porn user who continues unabated will often turn into an abuser of some kind.

Porn use in an abusive marriage may not lead to acts of sexual violence against a wife (though it often will). That is not what defines it as abusive. An abuser may use pornography in the same ways as many other men, but his heart overflows with entitlement, objectification, shame, and control. He will manipulate and use sex/pornography to get what he wants.

Control is a central element of abuse. An abuser will crave porn for the power he feels from it, not simply the gratification of voyeuristic desires. The control and power he craves will often manifest in the types of porn he watches, how he uses it, and in other nonsexual areas of life as well. Oftentimes, abusive husbands who use pornography will exhibit some of the following behaviors:

- He demands sex.
- He threatens using porn if he doesn't get what he wants from her: "If you don't have sex, with me I'm going to look at porn," or "If you don't do _____ I'll watch porn." He may threaten extramarital relations: "If you don't do _____ I'll find someone else who will."
- He may abandon sex with his wife, only getting sexual gratification from pornography.
- He forces his wife to do sexual acts that she is uncomfortable with.
- Sex is primarily about satisfying him, his desires, not pleasing his wife. It is another form of objectifying his wife and not treating her as a person, equally valuable and made in the image of God.
- He uses pornography as a menu of sexual acts he would like his wife to perform.
- He punishes her for not complying with his sexual desires.
- He may force/coerce her to watch pornography.

- He may force her to make "homemade porn." If she complies, he will also often use those pornographic images against her. For example, he may threaten, "If you tell anyone, I'll show this to your parents (boss, friends, pastor, kids, etc.)."
- He may watch violent porn. This will often lead to acts of violence in the sexual relationship.
- He derives pleasure from seeing his wife denigrated, hurt, or fearful during sex.
- He may invite other people (and force his wife to allow other people) to participate in their sexual relationship.

8. If your husband demonstrates any of the behaviors or attitudes mentioned above and that makes you wonder whether you are in an abusive relationship, consider the following:

- Examine your spouse and your marriage to see if you notice any tendencies toward punishing, dominance, oppression, or control.
- Look at the questions listed above under number 2, and see whether any of these are present. If they are, I encourage you to reach out for help from the places mentioned above.
- If you are in immediate danger, please reach out to the National Domestic Abuse Hotline: https://www.thehotline.org/.

Appendix 2
Ministry after Porn

EVEN IF YOU don't have a "ministry job," I want to encourage you to read this appendix—both for your good and for others who you might have a chance to minister to. Even if you don't work in "vocational ministry," many of the lies that Satan uses to take pastors out of the pulpit can be turned on you to keep you from doing the good works that God has called you to do. Your husband may have stepped out of volunteer ministry because his struggle with porn left him thinking that God would never use someone who struggles with sexual sin to serve the church. The pages that follow will encourage repentant individuals to reengage in the ministry God has called them to. God may also put you in the path of a pastor, missionary, or someone else serving in vocational ministry who struggles with porn (or is married to someone who does). You can then use the comfort God has given you in your husband's struggle to help others in theirs (2 Corinthians 1:3–4). So, whoever you are, please keep reading.

I cowrote this appendix with my husband to help you and your spouse think through questions that can arise when someone serving in ministry struggles with pornography. We've been married for over nineteen years and have navigated many phases of ministry life. Together we've attended seminary and have served the church both on a voluntary basis and through full-time vocational ministry (pastoring in the local church and directing parachurch organizations). When we first started out, good advice was sparse for individuals struggling with pornography— and especially sparse for women whose husbands were struggling with pornography. There were occasions that we needed help but didn't know where to turn for guidance. So we want to provide this appendix to answer some of the tough questions that we had ourselves and have since heard from others.

Question 1: Does any pornography use automatically disqualify a person from leadership in Christian ministry?

If you have read this book, then you understand that we do not believe pornography use automatically disqualifies someone from leadership in Christian ministry. If you skipped ahead to this section without reading the book, now you know. Of course, giving the simple answer, "No" to this question would not suffice. The question is more complex and requires further explanation.

Before we delve deeper into this question, we want to make it clear that we do not speak for every Christian, nor do we claim to have absolute authority on this matter. There are many godly men and women who will disagree with the position we take. You, the reader, must weigh our words (and the words of those who disagree) against the only infallible, fully authoritative source of knowledge we have—the Bible. We will do our best to explain our position and support it biblically. If you are on staff at a church or considering a ministry role at a church where the leadership/ church policies differ from the position articulated below, then you need to submit to that leadership/church policy. Feel free to use our material to try to persuade them otherwise, but do not create division in the church over this issue. Respect and submit to the authorities that God has placed over that local congregation whether you agree with them or not. If you cannot do so in good conscience, then you should not accept a position in that church, and you should consider moving to another ministry if you must.

There are so many variables at play in each person's situation that it would be impossible for us to address every single one. You need to have open and honest conversations about your particular situation with your spouse and the spiritual shepherds in your life. This is necessary whether you are in ministry already or are considering future ministry options. You need to remove yourself as the primary decision maker in these conversations and be willing to submit to the wisdom of your pastor/elders (Hebrews 13:17). You need to be honest about the amount (frequency and duration of each incident, length of time this has been going on) and type (photos, videos, hetero, homo, child, or violent, etc.) of pornography you are consuming. You need to disclose the steps you have taken to battle this sin, the steps you have taken to undermine your battle, and the ways you have deceived those around you. This is important knowledge to help you and your church family battle your pornography use and decide whether or not you should be a ministry leader. Some types of pornography use are illegal and would necessitate the involvement of legal authorities. If the spiritual shepherds in your life do not feel equipped to assess your situation, they can consult a wise biblical counselor. Solomon SoulCare offers consulting services to counselors, pastors, and ministries. If the leadership surrounding you is unsure of how to proceed, they can visit https://solomonsoulcare.com/ to schedule a consultation. You can also visit the Biblical Counseling Coalition's website (https://www.biblicalcounselingcoalition.org/), which has a "Find a Counselor" page that lists many biblical counselors and links to other organizations that have counselor listings.

As mentioned above, we do not believe that pornography use automatically disqualifies someone from leadership in Christian ministry. What lies at the center of our concern is the state and inclination of your heart toward your sin and your Savior. The qualifications of elder/pastor in 1 Timothy 3 and Titus 1 must be consulted and used to evaluate you and your qualifications for those specific roles, but other passages should be brought to bear to help you (and others around you) consider your heart. These verses include Matthew 3:8, 5:6; Luke 3:8; Acts 26:20; Romans 7; 2 Corinthians 7; Galatians 5; and Philippians 2.

With these passages in mind, you and the shepherds of your local church need to consider the following questions:

1. What is the general inclination of your heart? Are you generally moving toward Christ and desiring to be more like him?
2. Do you genuinely hate your sin and long to be rid of it (Romans 7)?
3. Do you brazenly pursue your lust for pornography?
4. Is there genuine brokenness over your sin and a desire to forsake it and move toward Jesus (2 Corinthians 7)?
5. Looking at the totality of your life, which do you generally manifest—the deeds of the flesh or the fruit of the Spirit (Galatians 5)?
6. Do you hunger and thirst for righteousness (Matthew 5:6)?
7. Are you willing to humbly submit to the instruction, accountability measures, and oversight of your spiritual shepherds (Philippians 2; Hebrews 13)?
8. Are you actively seeking out ways to undermine, thwart, or skirt around the accountability measures in your life?
9. Is there evidence of genuine repentance in your life, in both attitude and action (Matthew 3:8; Luke 3:8; 2 Corinthians 7)?
10. Are you willing to involve others in the accountability process with an open and welcoming heart?

These questions are designed to reveal deeper heart attitudes rather than mere behavioral responses. Some people will appear repentant for a season as they conform to the external constraints imposed upon them. However, if their hearts are not genuinely transformed, they will inevitably return to pornography. Left unchecked, it is likely they will move beyond pornography into deeper sexual sins. If there is pride, refusal to be fully open and honest, a lack of desire to repent, or resistance to outside accountability and help, then those who are in a shepherding role should be concerned and consider steps to remove this person from ministry. Those who are genuinely repentant will likely still struggle, but they will also experience growth toward Christlikeness. There should be evidence of brokenness over sin, commitment to forsake the sin, a humble desire for oversight and accountability, and active demonstrations of repentance and growth over time.

When you consider the qualifications of an elder from 1 Timothy 3 and Titus 1, the words *above reproach* and *blameless* stand out as glaring condemnations for those who struggle with pornography use. While a full exegesis of these passages is outside the scope of this book, I want to offer these words of encouragement from one commentator discussing these words in Titus 1:6, 7:

> The only two other New Testament passages that contain this word suggest another possibility for explaining what Paul has in mind. First, Paul assures the Corinthians that Jesus Christ "will also keep you firm to the end, so that you will be blameless on the day of our Lord Jesus Christ" (1 Cor 1:8). Paul is not saying the Corinthians are presently perfect; his epistle to them is proof of the contrary. They are not even blameless in Paul's assessment, from a doctrinal and ethical point of view. He is rather speaking of them as believers "in Christ." As those who have believed and received the grace of the gospel (see 1 Cor 1:4–6), they possess a righteousness through faith that assures them of God's present, as well as eschatological, exoneration. They are blameless in God's sight by virtue of the sufficiency of Christ's death for their sake.[1]

When God calls pastors/elders to be "above reproach" it is not a requirement of perfection, nor is it something that people can create in themselves. It is only something that is accomplished in the completed work of Christ. If your spouse is truly running to and relying on Christ to be transformed, then there is hope and assurance that he will grow (Philippians 1:6).

Question 2: What if a person struggles with pornography use multiple times in his life? Does that disqualify him from pastoral ministry?

This is a follow-up question to the first one. We would apply similar principles as in our answer above, but encourage the church leaders/shepherds involved to examine this person's history more carefully. The primary concern is whether or not the person is genuinely repentant and seeking to grow or whether the repeated struggle with porn is evidence that his heart is not inclined toward God but toward self and feeding this sin.

Some additional questions to ask in these situations:

1. How many times has this been an issue?
2. Tell us about each period of pornography use in the past. What led to each incident (context of what was going on in life, what preceded the initial return that time— accidentally stumbled across enticing images, actively pursued pornography, etc.)? How long did it last? What kinds of pornography were you viewing (see questions in the previous section)?
3. What led to your sin being exposed (was it voluntary disclosure or involuntary discovery)?
4. What did you do at that time to forsake your sin?
5. Were there attempts to undermine your accountability?
6. How did you grow or change between incidents?

This sixth question is a difficult question to wrestle through, and we must ask God for wisdom in discerning the heart of the person struggling with pornography. The goal is to seek to understand this person's heart from God's perspective. Is this a believer who is genuinely struggling and growing or someone who keeps returning to this sin because it is what he truly desires? You want to see signs that a person is growing. This change is manifest through decreasing duration, longer periods of abstaining from pornography, and growth toward Christ. However, we must be careful not to create arbitrary timelines or measurements of repentance (i.e., "three strikes you're out").

It is important to note that pornography use can disqualify a person from pastoral ministry. For instance, a pattern of chronic pornography use would violate the qualifications of an elder in Titus 1:7–8. A person who wrestles in this way is not demonstrating self-control, is not disciplined, and is not above reproach.

Question 3: We are seminary students, and my husband struggles with pornography. What should accountability look like in this phase of life? Should we even be pursuing ministry?

Accountability for each phase of life should include people who are close to you in proximity and those who are well acquainted with you and your struggle. Preferably there is overlap, but in seasons where you are transient (seminary) or new to a place (landing in a new ministry), you are going to rely most on those who have known you for some time even though they may be far off. However, you need to be proactive in your search for someone where you gather regularly for worship who will provide you in-person accountability. If you have not had accountability in the past, then you need to start *now* wherever you are. When you are serving in a ministry or on staff with a ministry, it is essential that someone in leadership over you is made aware of the problem as soon as possible. This means that if you have not disclosed this already, you need to make a plan (preferably with your spouse and counselor) to meet with your pastor/supervisor/board of directors member and share openly and honestly about your struggle.

This also means that when you are moving to a new position you need to be forthright about your struggle and pertinent sexual history. This will actually be an excellent way for you to clarify whether this is a good ministry for you to be a part of and establish a strong, transparent, trusting relationship early in your ministry. It will alleviate any fear or worry that your sin will be discovered. This will eliminate any doubt about whether or not you would have gotten the job if they really knew you. It will kill the doubts that creep in whispering that somehow your sin is the source of difficulty in ministry. All these thoughts will assail you in ministry as ammunition of the enemy to undermine what God wants to accomplish in and through you.

If you are currently a seminary student struggling with porn and you are wondering whether you/we should even pursue ministry, this can only be answered in the context of community. This is a question that your local church family can help you answer. They will only be able to apply wisdom to this question if you are fully transparent with them—they need to know who you really are (and how you really struggle) to confirm your calling to ministry (or encourage you to take a break from seminary in order to pursue personal growth). You need to honestly disclose every aspect of your history with porn use/sexual sin with a few wise leaders in your church (the questions listed in question 1 of this appendix and accountability questions in chapters 4 and 7 are good places to start), then ask those leaders to help you discern whether or not seminary is the best place for you right now. If you are considering seminary, these transparent conversations will prepare you for conversations that will need to take place in future ministry interviews. If you are currently a seminary student, those hard conversations need to happen without delay.

Question 4: We are currently in the process of interviewing with churches for ministry positions. We wonder if, when, how, and to who should we disclose the struggle with pornography.

This is a tricky question because it doesn't have one clear answer for every situation. The answer will come through discernment, prayer, and seeking wise counsel. One thing that is absolutely clear is that before you accept a new ministry position, someone in leadership needs to know. In most cases, we wouldn't recommend someone put this on a resume or other documentation that is requested in the early phases of the hiring process. It is better disclosed face-to-face so that clarifying questions can be asked and opportunities for confusion are minimized. As you proceed through the process you will likely be interviewed via telephone or video chat, and then have one or two in-person interviews (this is especially true with churches). As the process progresses, you will begin to build relationships with the people involved in leadership in the church. This will help you gain comfort and wisdom about when to disclose your struggle and to whom. Pray specifically for wisdom regarding this matter and recruit others to pray for you (your wife, current accountability allies, etc.). Trust God to open up the opportunity—then take it. We can't give you a detailed time line, but we insist that you do it before you accept the position, as we discussed in answering the previous question.

Question 5: As a pastor, should my accountability come from inside or outside the church that I am pastoring?

The answer is both. Ideally, every pastor should have men within the church and outside the church who know him intimately and can be sources of encouragement and accountability in all matters of life, including his struggle with sexual temptations. Many pastors avoid accountability within the church because they are afraid that their sin will be used against them or that people will lose respect for them as a shepherd. But when has our obedience ever been dependent upon whether or not others will behave appropriately? When is it ever good to make decisions based on fear? When has God ever called his undershepherds to pretend to be something they are not or to act as though they have no sin? Where does Scripture say that there is a lesser expectation or demand for obedience from the leaders of the church than the other members? Quite the opposite, God's Word says that leaders will be held to a higher account (Matthew 13:12; Luke 12:48; James 3:1). God tells us he has not given us a spirit of fear but of power (2 Timothy 1:7). God's Word tells us that if we say we have no sin or have not sinned we are self-deceived, liars, we make God out to be a liar, and his word is not in us (1 John 1:8–10). God's Word calls us to faithfulness despite the accusations of others, both true and false.

We convince ourselves that if people know about our sin it will damage our ministry and the church. But which is more damaging—revealing the truth and demonstrating how God calls people to overcome sin or hiding it and pretending we are somehow above the sins that are common to every man? What is more damaging—shining light into the dark places or pretending they don't exist and allowing sin to fester and grow there until it is discovered? What is more damaging—a pastor who is humble and acknowledges his sin and dependence upon God and the work of Christ or the one who promotes a false vision of self-righteousness and independence? Which has been more damaging to the church—pastors who walked in humility or those whose pride led them to public failure? Think about your own experience with other ministry leaders. What did it do to you when a pastor was willing to be open and honest about his sin struggles, his weakness, and his dependence upon Christ, His Spirit, the Word of God, and the church? On the other hand, what does it do to you each time you hear of another church leader who has fallen from his false pedestal, tearing down his ministry, tearing apart his family, and disgracing the name of Christ?

You are living proof of the statistics we cited before. The question is not whether or not pastors struggle with porn; they do, you do. The question is what are we going to do about it? Silence on the matter has not resolved the problem; instead, it has likely exacerbated it. We need to speak openly and honestly about this problem. I am not suggesting that you share your personal sin publicly, but you should not allow your personal sin to prevent you from dealing publicly with a sin that is rampant in the church. As mentioned in the accountability chapter, I do encourage you to share your personal sin with a few trustworthy people within the leadership of the church. If you can't do that privately with someone in your church, how can you hope to be part of the solution for not only your own struggle but for the infection spreading throughout the church around the world?

Question 6: I am (or my spouse is) a staff pastor/parachurch ministry employee/unpaid elder who struggles with pornography. No one in my congregation/parachurch ministry knows about this struggle. How and to whom should I confess this sin/go to for help?

Go first to somebody in leadership (the lead pastor if that is not you) and also to somebody with whom you have a strong relationship. Those two realities may reside in the same person, but if they don't, you need to have this conversation with multiple people. It is essential that someone in leadership knows about the struggle because they are charged with the care of all the sheep in the flock. That means they need to know about potential threats to the local body—which includes your struggle with porn. That person is also going to hold you accountable personally and professionally. Having a strong relationship with someone in the church to whom you are personally accountable is necessary because that relationship's ground is already broken up, plowed, and prepared for growth and flourishing. You already know he loves you and you love him. This will make it easier for you to be honest, real, and raw with him. It also increases the likelihood that he will demonstrate true Christlike love, grace, and mercy toward you and lovingly confront you when necessary.

Question 7: I am a pastor/elder and another pastor at my church or in my sphere of influence has recently confessed pornography use. What early steps do I need to take in this situation?

First of all, thank God that he has led this brother to share with you. Second, encourage your brother that he has made a significant step toward repentance and growth in Christ. Affirm your love and appreciation for him. Acknowledge the courage it took to come to you and confess this sin. Through this and your continued love and friendship you are putting flesh to the grace, mercy, and love of Christ described in the Scriptures. After you have done these things, your next steps will depend on your relationship to one another and the roles that you play in your local church contexts. If you are in separate churches, you will want to encourage him to confess his sin to another leader in his congregation. You can use the answers in this book to point out the need for and value of immediate accountability in the local church. You can also offer to accompany him for this conversation and commit to being an additional relationship for external accountability if that is wise for you and him.

If you both serve on staff at the same church, your next steps (after the first two mentioned above) will depend on your roles in the church and whether or not your church has policies in place that offer guidance for this situation. If there are policies in place, follow them. Whether or not you agree with them, trying to change them in the midst of a disclosure is not wise.

If there aren't policies in place to follow and you are the lead pastor, we would encourage you to prayerfully begin the counseling process with this man and his wife (if he is married). You can use this book and its companion as guides to walk through the process. You will need to do some initial investigation to determine the level of struggle, the commitment to change, and whether or not removal from ministry is going to be necessary at this time. If you are unsure of how to proceed, https://solomonsoulcare.com/ offers consulting services to help counselors, pastors, and ministries navigate the aftermath of porn. If removal is not indicated, then recruit a counseling ally or ally couple and begin working with this pastor to foster resolute repentance in his life.

If there are no policies and you are not the lead pastor, then you need to encourage this pastor to confess to the lead pastor. Again, encourage him by accompanying him to the conversation (if he desires) and being willing to walk alongside him through this process and beyond.

Question 8: What should ongoing accountability look like for a pastor/ elder/ministry leader who struggles with pornography?

Ongoing accountability for a ministry leader is going to involve the same elements of accountability discussed throughout this book with a couple of additional measures. First, someone else who is a leader in the church must be a part of the accountability relationship. This is not essential for all church members, but it is for a leader.

A level of professional accountability must be in place for staff pastors/ministry leaders. A ministry leader's vocation can be at risk when he is struggling with pornography. Because of this he should not be left to himself to make the decision about his qualification for this role. At least one other person who is in a position of professional authority (able to take action to remove him if necessary) needs to be aware of his struggle and (at the least) maintain an active awareness of the accountability process. This can be a senior pastor if the individual is on staff with multiple pastors, an elder or member of the ruling board if he is the lead or solo pastor, or a member of the board of directors for parachurch ministry leaders.

Additionally, because of the often-transient nature of ministry jobs, pastors and ministry leaders who struggle with sexual temptation need external accountability from strong believers who know them well and are committed, lifetime friends. Often another minister who serves in a similar ministry will be a great ally. If the pastor is married, his wife should also be apprised of both of these relationships and be able to call on them at any time.

Question 9: As a ministry wife, what do I do if my husband refuses to seek help for his porn struggle? What if he begs me not to tell anyone? We don't have enough money in savings to face extreme financial hardship. What if I speak up and we lose our livelihood?

We've all seen public scandals that revealed a wife as complicit in her husband's sexual misdeeds. Each time a new one breaks I think the same thing: *Not on my watch—I won't ever make it easier for my husband to cover sexual sin!* The fact that you are taking time to read the answer to this question tells me that you probably have the same resolve. If you aren't sure that you would be willing to reveal your husband's sin if he refuses to do so, please ask yourself the same question I asked you earlier: Who do I hope to become? Your response to this crisis will either be a step away from Jesus or a faithful step indicating deep dependence on your savior. There's no neutral course of action. What's more important to you right now—temporary comforts or being close to Jesus? What I am asking you to do might be one of the scariest things God ever requires of you. I promise God will give you the strength and wisdom you need, if you ask for wisdom and trust him to provide. If you haven't already read chapter 6, "Abigail: A Wise Woman Who Did What She Could," please do; you will find additional, emboldening help there.

The question we are thinking through is an extremely important one. You are in an intimidating situation. Your husband's/your concern that he will potentially face disciplinary measures at work is reasonable, and it comes with the temptation to ignore or even cover up blatant sexual sin because bringing it to light will put your family's reputation and livelihood on the line. Many pastors and ministry leaders have been fired for porn use (and other forms of sexual sin). It will be painful and stressful to uncover his sin against his will and await whatever consequences may come. If you have good reason to believe that his employment or your housing are in jeopardy, it is reasonable to first take steps to provide for your family. This does not mean putting off confessing his sin for an extended period while you stockpile money or search for and secure comparable income through new employment; it means securing necessities for the immediate future. This could look like calling your parents or a trusted friend and asking them for financial help or temporary housing in the event that your husband's employer does call for his immediate removal.

Before you reveal his sin, it would also be appropriate to urge your husband toward repentance with a statement such as the following:

> I will not become complicit in your sin by helping you cover it up. I love Jesus and I love you too much to let you continue down this path. I would rather lose our home and every material possession we have so that we can go to bed each night with the peace that comes from obeying God than commit sin to avoid difficulty. I want to encourage you to confess your sin to (name of a person in spiritual authority over him), in order to establish a plan to fight this sin. I'd like you to talk to him by (name a specific date, discussed with your counselor).

If your husband refuses to confess and turn from his sin, and the time frame passes, go back to him, and let him know he has left you no choice but to bring his sin to the attention of the people in authority over him. You can also share with your husband some of the encouragement you have gained from this book. Remind him that God cares for him and will use this confession for his good. Let him know you are praying that God gives him the courage to confess his sin.

God will be with you through this confrontation. Other women have walked this path of brave obedience. Pleasing God often means displeasing people. This is an opportunity for you to become like Sarah by doing good and not fearing anything that is frightening (1 Peter 3:6). You have an obligation before your Heavenly Father to do spiritual good to your spouse by confronting and exposing his sin. To leave your husband trapped and alone in his secret sin without offering accountability from your local church family would be unloving toward him, negligent toward the church, and unfaithful toward God. As you seek to honor God, he will sustain you. God will provide for you. There are far more valuable things at risk than a job, an income, or even your family's home. Your husband's soul could be on the line. If he continues to hide his sin and refuses to repent, this is potential evidence that he lacks saving faith. Ask yourself, *Which is ultimately better—to lose my most valuable material possessions and give my husband an opportunity to gain victory over the sin that wants to eat him alive or to keep my bank account balance steady and give sin an opportunity to master my husband?* Eternity is long; this life is short. God has given you a priceless opportunity to serve him by exposing your husband's sin. Take heart and take action!

Question 10: We feel like we are living a lie. How should we deal with feelings of hypocrisy while we continue to serve in a ministry setting and fight an ongoing battle against porn?

Our question is why do you feel like you are living a lie? It's possible that you feel like you are living a lie because you are living a lie. Does anyone in your church, parachurch ministry, community group, circle of Christian friends, or extended family know about this struggle with porn? If the answer is no, then your feelings are correct. You are living a lie. One of the greatest gifts that accountability bestows upon the one who comes confessing sin is the comfort of being known. Psalm 139:1–12 reminds us that we can't go anywhere and be hidden from the gaze of God.

He knows and sees us. That's one thing that makes the gospel so glorious. God came for us with full knowledge of who we are and what we've done. God always truly knows us and he still has bountiful compassion. So much that he sent Jesus to die for our sins because he knew our plight. We can't accept Jesus until we are willing to admit that we are sinners. It shouldn't come as a great surprise to your Christian friends when you confess sin to them. They are sinners too, and they have already recognized sin within themselves and admitted that to God. The church should be the first place where people feel comfortable admitting the specifics of their sins. This isn't always the case, and the church needs to ask how have we created an environment where people don't feel that they can be honest about their struggles? Could it be that you need to lead by example? Perhaps if you start by confessing your sexual sin to a few people at your church who can offer you care and accountability, this may be the catalyst for making your church a shelter for repentant souls. What if your church comes to be known as a place that is marked by consistent repentance rather than hypocrisy? If that sounds appealing, you need to set a good example. Take the lead in making it such a place by consistently repenting and seeking out accountability for yourself.

Maybe in the past you confessed your sin to God, people in spiritual authority over you, your spouse, and one or two accountability partners, yet you still feel like a hypocrite. Do you continue to have an ongoing, honest conversation with those same people about your struggle with sexual sin? Are you currently hiding sins from them and/or now refusing to confess to God? If you are maintaining each of these relationships with honesty, real-time confession, and repentance, then there aren't sin skeletons in your closet. In this case you are not a hypocrite. Everyone in your life does not need to know about all your sin struggles in order for you to avoid the label of hypocrite. People who are part of the solution need to be aware of the problem, not everyone else. You are forgiven and loved by God. Your friends also truly know you, and they love you too. Ask God to use your mistakes for good. He can do that. He does do that! Look for ways to use vulnerability and authenticity to bless others, even if it creates discomfort for you. Jesus set aside comfort for the good of the church. Let him be your best example as you try to do the same.

If you have these open honest relationships and still feel like a hypocrite, it may be because you believe the lie that, as a spiritual leader, you will somehow be able to keep the Word of God perfectly. We may not often say it exactly this way, but that is one outworking of a prideful heart that is forgetting the fundamentals of the gospel. You need a savior because you can't keep the Word of God perfectly. This means you continue to hold up God's standards, while also acknowledging your inability to attain those standards. Continue to be honest about your shortcomings and allow them to foster daily dependence on the grace of Jesus Christ.

Question 11: I picked up this book because I am dating/engaged to someone who is preparing for full time ministry. He struggles with pornography—what advice do you have for me?

First, we want to alleviate some pressure from you. You are not under any obligation to marry this person. You have not made a covenant commitment, and you can freely exit this relationship if you so choose with a clear conscience before God and people. Before you rush to this conclusion, it is important to remember that there's not a perfect person out there for you to marry. Everyone struggles with sin. It's good that you are seeing some of his struggles now. It's good to go into marriage (if you do) with a realistic understanding of who you are marrying and what tempts him.

The second thing we want you to understand is that you aren't the solution to his porn problem. He doesn't look at porn because he wants/needs to have sex with you but can't yet. He looks at porn because he lacks self-control. Your honeymoon won't be a wand that waves over his porn issues and turns them magically into contented married sex. The best indicator that your husband won't struggle with porn during marriage is that he put aside porn before marriage and that he exhibited sexual self-control when he was dating/engaged to you. Does he do this now? Do the two of you treat each other's sexual purity with dignity and care, or do you find yourselves overstepping boundaries? Don't be flattered by his premarital sexual advances. They are serious red flags indicating sexual sin ahead in marriage. Seek counsel now. Seek accountability now. Be humble, step up, and be the first one to confess that you haven't honored the sexual boundaries that God established for your good. See if he follows suit. Ask someone in spiritual authority over you—your parents if they are mature Christians or your friends—to help you maintain agreed-upon boundaries. Don't spend time alone in places that create an atmosphere for compromise. Ask him to safeguard himself from the temptations of porn through regular in-person accountability, pastoral oversight, firewalls, accountability software on all his devices, and password protection. See if he is willing to shore up areas of temptation. If he responds humbly, you are well on the way to becoming his best ally, and you can enter marriage with a plan of attack that will help you fight this sin together. If he refuses to change and grow, you have good reason to walk away from this relationship.

The question is not whether he will sin after you are married—he will and so will you. The thing you need to look for is how he responds to being confronted with his sin and whether or not he confesses his sins willingly. Is he a humble sinner or an arrogant one? Does he defend his actions, hide his sin, make excuses for himself, or manipulate you into sinning with him? Or is he humble, honest, and willing to get help? Humble people confess sin and seek help. Arrogant people think they can deal with it alone and that no one needs to know.

You need to possess and model this same humility by bringing other older, wiser Christians into your relationship and asking them to help you evaluate the questions listed above. Don't assume that you have the wisdom and experience to observe his behavior alone and decide for yourself. You need wise spiritual oversight right now just as much as your boyfriend/fiancé does.

If you marry him, you will become each other's lifelong ally in the fight against sin. Is he willing to fight his sin now? Can you envision yourself fighting sexual sin alongside him for the next 60 years? A lot of the best things that come out of a good marriage happen because both people are willing to get in the trenches and go to battle for each other.

So is he a fighter or a defector? How did you find out about this struggle with porn? Did your boyfriend/fiancé confess it willingly? If he volunteered the information, he is more likely a fighter. Did you stumble across it, catching him unaware? If so, he may be a defector. Are there other people in his and your life who know the full extent of the struggle? Our advice to someone who is repentant and showing that attitude—humbly submitting to outside help, struggling but growing, receiving counsel, pastoral oversight, and accountability, while also demonstrating sexual self-control toward you—would be to encourage you both to keep up the good work. It sounds like you are on the right track. In this scenario, encourage your boyfriend/fiancé to continue to fight his sexual sin and quickly confess failures.

On the other hand, if your boyfriend/fiancé is arrogant—secretive about his porn struggle, doesn't seem broken over his sin, isn't currently pursuing counsel, pastoral oversight, and accountability, and/or is not demonstrating self-control in his physical relationship with you, then we would encourage you to take a step back in the relationship. It would be fine to end the relationship now, or you could give him some time and space to exhibit growth and change before considering whether or not your relationship should end or advance.

Is Pornography Use Grounds for Divorce?

BEFORE WE ANSWER the question of whether or not pornography use is grounds for divorce, I want to encourage you to pursue marriage counseling with a biblical counselor if divorce has been brought up by either you or your husband. Divorce is no small matter. If either of you is contemplating divorce, or if the threat of divorce has been thrown around in your fights, you need to seek marriage counseling with a biblical counselor as soon as possible.

To a serious degree, porn use violates the exclusivity of the marriage covenant. It is a form of sexual immorality. At the same time, porn use is something less than an adulterous relationship, because it lacks physical or emotional connection to another person. There's a spectrum of sexual sin that moves from lustful thoughts to adulterous relationships. Pornography use lands somewhere between those two sins. But don't take this to mean that God and your husband are in some kind of boy's club together where your husband is allowed to have his porn and his wife too, without relational or spiritual repercussions. One of the reasons I devote many pages of this book to empowering women to wisely seek accountability for their husbands (even if it's against his will) is because sexual sin is insidious. If your husband is struggling with porn and he's unrepentant, porn will eventually master him.

In time he may outgrow these visually oriented cravings and seek increasingly brazen forms of sexual expression to fulfill his longings. Porn unconfessed doesn't relent or lead solely to a little more porn—it often leads to violent porn, child porn, sexting someone from work, online sexual chats with strangers, strip clubs, prostitutes, and affairs. Those things are all grounds for separation and potentially lead to divorce. If your husband has not yet exhibited repentance, but also hasn't ventured down any of these increasingly deviant roads, praise God that he has thus far been kept from greater destruction. Then seek out accountability without delay (for more on this see chapters 4 and 7), and commit to ongoing transparency in your local church so they can pray for you and support you as you wait on God. He's the only One who can change your husband's heart.

In short, Curtis and I believe that a spouse viewing pornography is not grounds for divorce because it is not the same as adultery. To show you why we have come to this conclusion, we will deconstruct the typical arguments used to support the idea that pornography use is an offense for which divorce is an acceptable end to the marriage. Looking at several different passages in the Bible that focus on Jesus's teaching regarding divorce and adultery, most people agree that adultery is grounds for divorce (Deuteronomy 24:1–4; Matthew 19:3–12; Mark 10:1–12; Luke 16:18). In Matthew 5:27–28 Jesus says, "You have heard that it was said, 'You shall not commit adultery.' But I say to you that everyone who looks at a woman with lustful intent has already committed adultery with her in his heart." As the argument goes, this makes lust (clearly including pornography) equal to adultery and therefore a divorceable offense.

Let's put this argument into a logical syllogism:

Adultery is a divorceable offense.

Pornography use is adultery.

Therefore, pornography use is a divorceable offense.

The problem lies in the second premise. This idea that pornography use is identical to adultery is faulty. Jesus does not say that lust and the act of adultery are identical sins and thus incur the same human/legal consequences.

We can see the problem with the logic if we place Matthew 5:27–28 back into its context. Just prior to this, Jesus uses the same argument demonstrating the connection between murder and anger/hatred. In verses 21–22 Jesus says, "You have heard that it was said to those of old, 'You shall not murder; and whoever murders will be liable to judgment.' But I say to you that everyone who is angry with his brother will be liable to judgment; whoever insults his brother will be liable to the council; and whoever says, 'You fool!' will be liable to the hell of fire." Applying the same logic as was used above, we see this syllogism:

> Murder is a legally punishable offense (jail or death penalty).
>
> Anger is murder.
>
> Therefore, anger is legally punishable with jail time or death.

Obviously, no one wants to start applying that text in this fashion. Our jails (and death-row) would be overflowing with inmates, and we would all be among those serving sentences.

We do not intend to undermine the seriousness of pornography; as we stated before, pornography use is a heinous sin, and we want to fight it. However, in this passage, Jesus was not trying to make literal statements about the legal consequences of sin; he was elevating people's awareness of the seriousness of sin and conveying that it is not merely how we act externally that matters. We don't need only externally constrained behavior; we need internally transformed hearts.

Another argument sometimes used to declare pornography a divorceable offense is rooted in the vocabulary Jesus uses in Matthew 5:32 and 19:3–9. When the Pharisees question Jesus on the lawfulness of a man divorcing his wife, Jesus first establishes the high value God places on marriage by stating, "Have you not read that he who created them from the beginning made them male and female, and said, 'Therefore a man shall leave his father and his mother and hold fast to his wife, and the two shall become one flesh'? So, they are no longer two but one flesh. What therefore God has joined together, let not man separate" (Matthew 19:4–6). When they press him on the question by pointing out the fact that Moses allowed men to divorce their wives (Deuteronomy 24:1–4) Jesus responds, "Because of your hardness of heart Moses allowed you to divorce your wives, but from the beginning it was not so. And I say to you: whoever divorces his wife, except for sexual immorality, and marries another, commits adultery" (Matthew 19:8–9). In these verses Jesus uses two terms to describe sexual sin *moicheia*, which is translated "adultery" and *porneia*, which is "sexual immorality." In normal usage, *moicheia* refers to sexual activity by a married person with someone besides his/her spouse.[1] *Porneia*, on the other hand, is a term with a broader semantic domain, including other forms of sexual sin such as prostitution, unchastity, and fornication.[2]

The logic flowing from the argument is this: If someone divorces for something other than *porneia*, then they commit adultery (*moicheia*); therefore, divorcing for *porneia* is allowed. Accepting this line of reason, we must answer the question, does pornography use qualify as *porneia*? And we must consider the following points to answer this question.

First, just because we get the word *pornography* from the word *porneia* does not mean that pornography necessarily qualifies as *porneia*. This is a common misstep people fall into when they do word studies as part of their Bible study. One example of this is when preachers say that God has "explosive power" because the word *dynamite* comes from the word *dunamis*, which is translated as "power" in the New Testament (ninety-two times in the English Standard Version). They are reading dynamite back into *dunamis*, but dynamite was not invented until hundreds of years after the New Testament was written.[3] Likewise, because *porneia* is the root word for what we call pornography today neither affirms nor denies that modern porn equals *porneia*.

Second, Jesus's response to the Pharisees leans toward a narrower limitation on divorce, not a more expansive position. We need to keep this in mind with any discussion of divorce and be on guard for people who seem to be rushing to divorce or approaching it with a flippant attitude.

Third, the term *porneia*, while including more sexual deviancy than only adultery, still describes sexual acts with another human being. Pornography that doesn't spill over into sexual activity with other people is more in line with what Jesus addressed in Matthew 5:27–28, which we discussed above.

Fourth, certain extreme cases of pornography use may come within the parameters of a divorceable offense. The case has been made that where pornography and masturbation has completely supplanted the sexual activity between a husband and wife, it violates the one-flesh relationship of marriage and therefore qualifies as adultery.[4]

Finally, as we mentioned above, unfettered, unaddressed, unrepentant pornography use will tend to spiral into worse sin, often turning into illicit sexual activity involving other people. Some types of pornography and inappropriate sexual behavior within marriage are illegal and bring with them legal consequences and potentially divorce, including child pornography, marital rape, sexual abuse in marriage, etc. Please consult appendix 1, "Porn and Abuse," for more information on this topic. Our encouragement to you is to allow others in your church, hopefully your biblical counselor, pastor, and other spiritual leaders, to help you make any decision regarding the ending of marriage. It is a difficult decision with weighty consequences that should not be entered into lightly. Invite others into the process of making that decision with you.

Remember, just because divorce is at times permissible does not mean it is mandatory. There are many people who pursue forgiveness and reconciliation even in instances of adultery. However, there are times when divorce is appropriate. We cannot outline each and every scenario here, nor can we speak directly to your individual situation, so please reach out for help and wisdom from people near you who know you.

Bibliography

Adamson, James B. *The Epistle of James*. The New International Commentary on the New Testament. Grand Rapids: Eerdmans Publishing, 1976.

Bailey, Kenneth E. *Through Peasant Eyes: A Literary-Cultural Approach to the Parables in Luke*. Combined ed. Grand Rapids: Eerdmans Publishing, 1983.

Baldwin, Joyce. *1 And 2 Samuel: An Introduction and Commentary*. Vol. 8. Tyndale Old Testament Commentaries. Downers Grove: InterVarsity Press, 1988.

Bergen, Robert D. *1, 2 Samuel*. The New American Commentary. Vol. 7. Nashville, TN: Broadman & Holman, 1996.

Carson, D. A. *Exegetical Fallacies*. 2nd ed. Grand Rapids: Baker Books, 1996.

Couric, Katie. "Is Violent Porn Changing Us?" Audio. Next Question with Katie Couric. Accessed September 26, 2019. https://podcasts.apple.com/us/podcast/is-violent-porn-changing-us/id1134154895?i=1000451338319.

Covenant Eyes. *Porn Stats: 250+ Facts, Quotes, and Statistics about Pornography Use (2018 Edition)*. Covenant Eyes, 2018. https://www.covenanteyes.com/pornstats/.

Danker, Frederick W., Walter Bauer, and William Arndt. *A Greek-English Lexicon of the New Testament and Other Early Christian Literature*. 3rd ed. Chicago: University of Chicago Press, 2000.

Ellis, E. Earle. *The Gospel of Luke*. New Century Bible Commentaries. Grand Rapids: Eerdmans Publishing, 1981.

Evans, Mary J. *New International Biblical Commentary*. Peabody, MA: Hendrickson Publishers, 2000.

Frame, John M. *The Doctrine of the Christian Life*. A Theology of Lordship. Phillipsburg, NJ: P & R Publishing, 2008.

Greer, Lainey. "The Utilization of a Theology of Human Embodiment to Address Body Image." PhD dissertation, The Southern Baptist Theological Seminary, 2021.

Gregoire, Sheila Wray, Rebecca Gregoire Lindenbach, and Joanna Sawatsky. *The Great Sex Rescue: The Lies You've Been Taught and How to Recover What God Intended*. Grand Rapids: Baker Books, a division of Baker Publishing Group, 2021.

Hiebert, D. Edmond. *James*. Chicago: Moody Press, 1992.

Jones, Robert D. *Pursuing Peace: A Christian Guide to Handling Our Conflicts*. Wheaton, IL: Crossway, 2012.

Kail, Thomas. *Hamilton: An American Musical*. Walt Disney Studios Motion Pictures, 2020.

Keil, Carl Friedrich, and Franz Delitzsch. *Biblical Commentary on The Books of Samuel*. Commentaries on the Old Testament. Grand Rapids: Eerdmans Publishing, 1963.

Kellemen, Robert W. *God's Healing for Life's Losses: How to Find Hope When You're Hurting*. Winona Lake, IN: BMH Books, 2010.

Keller, Timothy. "Sexual Love—If It's Not Expressed in an Exclusive, Life-Long Covenant Relationship—Is Dehumanizing." *Twitter*, March 31, 2021. https://twitter.com/timkellernyc/status/1377260394289500169.

Kent, Homer Austin. *Faith That Works: Studies in the Epistle of James*. New Testament Studies. Grand Rapids: Baker Book House, 1986.

Kistemaker, Simon. *The Parables of Jesus*. Grand Rapids: Baker Book House, 1980.

Kittel, Gerhard, Gerhard Friedrich, and Geoffrey William Bromiley, eds. *Theological Dictionary of the New Testament*. Grand Rapids: Eerdmans Publishing, 1985.

Lawrence, Brother. *The Practice of the Presence of God*. Westwood, NJ: Fleming H. Revell Company, 1958.

Moo, Douglas J. *The Letter of James*. The Pillar New Testament Commentary. Grand Rapids: Eerdmans Publishing, 2000.

Morris, Leon. *Luke*. Tyndale New Testament Commentaries. Vol. 3. Downers Grove, IL: Intervarsity Press, 2008.

Newheiser, Jim. *Marriage, Divorce, and Remarriage: Critical Questions and Answers*. Phillipsburg: P & R Publishing, 2017.

Ortlund, Dane Calvin. *Gentle and Lowly: The Heart of Christ for Sinners and Sufferers*. Wheaton: Crossway, 2020.

Peterson, Andrew. "Honesty, Truth, and Beauty: A Celebration of the Music of Rich Mullins." Presented at the Hutchmoot, Franklin, TN, October 11, 2019.

Piper, John. "Luke 7:36–50, Part 2: God's Love for the Worst." Desiring God, September 24, 2015. https://www.desiringgod.org/labs/gods-love-for-the-worst.

Powlison, David. *Making All Things New: Restoring Joy to the Sexually Broken*. Wheaton, IL: Crossway, 2017.

Strickland, Darby. "How to Discern True Repentance When Serious Sin Has Occurred." *Journal of Biblical Counseling* 34, no. 3, 2020: 30–47.

Tiede, Vicki. *When Your Husband Is Addicted to Pornography: Healing Your Wounded Heart*. Greensboro, NC: New Growth Press, 2012.

Viars, Stephen. *Overcoming Bitterness: Moving from Life's Greatest Hurts to a Life Filled with Joy*. Grand Rapids: Baker Books, a division of Baker Publishing Group, 2021.

Vos, Howard Frederic. *1, 2 Samuel: Bible Study Commentary*. Bible Study Commentary Series. Grand Rapids: Zondervan, 1983.

Vroegop, Mark. *Dark Clouds, Deep Mercy: Discovering the Grace of Lament*. Wheaton, IL: Crossway, 2019.

Waititi, Taika. *JoJo Rabbit*. Fox Searchlight Pictures, 2019.

Wolf, Richard. *The General Epistles of James & Jude*. Contemporary Commentaries. Wheaton, IL: Tyndale House Publishers, 1969.

Yarbrough, Robert W. *The Letters to Timothy and Titus*. The Pillar New Testament Commentary. Grand Rapids: Eerdmans Publishing, 2018.

Endnotes

Introduction

1. Timothy Keller (@timkellernyc), "Sexual love—if it's not expressed in an exclusive, life-long covenant relationship—is dehumanizing," Twitter, March 31, 2021, 10:04 a.m., https://twitter.com/timkellernyc/status/1377260394289500169.

2. Ron DeHass, "What Are the Most Up-to-Date Stats on Pornography?" Covenant Eyes, accessed August 9, 2021, https://www.covenant eyes.com/pornstats/.

Chapter 2

1. Robert W. Kellemen, *God's Healing for Life's Losses: How to Find Hope When You're Hurting* (Winona Lake, IN: BMH Books, 2010), 18.

2. Kellemen, *God's Healing*, 55.

3. Mark Vroegop, *Dark Clouds, Deep Mercy: Discovering the Grace of Lament* (Wheaton, IL: Crossway, 2019), 30.

4. Vroegop, *Dark Clouds*, 21.

5. Vroegop, *Dark Clouds*, 26.

6. Vroegop, *Dark Clouds*, 29.

7. Vroegop, *Dark Clouds*, 60.

8. Vroegop, *Dark Clouds*, 29.

9. Vicki Tiede, *When Your Husband Is Addicted to Pornography: Healing Your Wounded Heart* (Greensboro, NC: New Growth Press, 2012), 174.

Chapter 3

1. Vicki Tiede, *When Your Husband Is Addicted to Pornography: Healing Your Wounded Heart* (Greensboro, NC: New Growth Press, 2012), 84.

2. Sheila Wray Gregoire, Rebecca Gregoire Lindenbach, and Joanna Sawatsky, *The Great Sex Rescue: The Lies You've Been Taught and How to Recover What God Intended* (Grand Rapids, MI: Baker Books, 2021), 106.

3. David Powlison, *Making All Things New: Restoring Joy to the Sexually Broken* (Wheaton, IL: Crossway, 2017), 41.

4. Gregoire, Lindenbach, and Sawatsky, *The Great Sex Rescue*, 114–15.

5. Lainey Greer, "The Utilization of a Theology of Human Embodiment to Address Body Image" (PhD diss., The Southern Baptist Theological Seminary, 2021), 149.

Chapter 4

1. Sheila Wray Gregoire, Rebecca Gregoire Lindenbach, and Joanna Sawatsky, *The Great Sex Rescue: The Lies You've Been Taught and How to Recover What God Intended* (Grand Rapids, MI: Baker Books, 2021), 186–87.

Chapter 5

1. Mary J. Evans, *New International Biblical Commentary* (Peabody, MA: Hendrickson, 2000), 113.

2. Howard Frederic Vos, *1, 2 Samuel: Bible Study Commentary*, Bible Study Commentary Series (Grand Rapids, MI: Zondervan, 1983), 84.

3. Robert D. Bergen, *1, 2 Samuel*, The New American Commentary Vol. 7 (Nashville, TN: Broadman & Holman, 1996), 245.

4. Evans, *New International Biblical Commentary*, 113–14.

5. Vos, *1, 2 Samuel*, 84.

6. Richard Wolf, *The General Epistles of James & Jude*, Contemporary Commentaries (Wheaton, IL: Tyndale House Publishers, 1969), 65.

7. D. Edmond Hiebert, *James* (Chicago: Moody Press, 1992), 69, quotes Robert Johnstone, *Lectures Exegetical and Practical on the Epistle of James* (Grand Rapids: Baker, 1954), 78.

8. Wolf, *The General Epistles of James & Jude*, 15.

9. James B. Adamson, *The Epistle of James*, The New International Commentary on the New Testament (Grand Rapids: Eerdmans, 1976), 154.

10. Wolf, *The General Epistles of James & Jude*, 64–65.

11. Homer Austin Kent, *Faith That Works: Studies in the Epistle of James*, New Testament Studies (Grand Rapids: Baker Book House, 1986), 135.

12. Hiebert, *James*, 210.

13. Kent, *Faith That Works*, 135.

14. Hiebert, *James*, 211.

15. Hiebert, *James*, 211.

16. Wolf, *The General Epistles of James & Jude*, 65.

17. Hiebert, *James*, 211.

18. Hiebert, *James*, 211.

19. Hiebert, *James*, 212.

20. Hiebert, *James*, 212.

21. Hiebert, *James*, 212.

22. Kent, *Faith That Works*, 137.

23. Douglas J. Moo, *The Letter of James*, The Pillar New Testament Commentary (Grand Rapids: Eerdmans, 2000), 57.

Chapter 6

1. Robert D. Bergen, *1, 2 Samuel*, The New American Commentary Vol. 7 (Nashville, TN: Broadman & Holman, 1996), 248.

2. Taika Waititi, *JoJo Rabbit* (Fox Searchlight Pictures, 2019).

3. Bergen, *1, 2 Samuel*, 249.

Chapter 7

1. Andrew Peterson, "Honesty, Truth, and Beauty: A Celebration of the Music of Rich Mullins" (presentation at Hutchmoot, Franklin, TN, October 11, 2019).

2. Peterson, "Honesty, Truth, and Beauty."

3. Kenneth E. Bailey, *Through Peasant Eyes: A Literary-Cultural Approach to the Parables in Luke* (Grand Rapids, MI: Eerdmans, 1983, 11.

4. Katie Couric, "Is Violent Porn Changing Us?," audio, Next Question with Katie Couric, accessed September 26, 2019, https://pod casts.apple.com/us/podcast/is-violent-porn-changing-us/id113415 4895?i=1000451338319.

Chapter 8

1. *Hamilton: An American Musical*, directed by Thomas Kail (Walt Disney Studios Motion Pictures, 2020) accessed on Disney+ streaming platform 7/4/2020.

2. Vicki Tiede, *When Your Husband Is Addicted to Pornography: Healing Your Wounded Heart* (Greensboro, NC: New Growth Press, 2012), 120.

3. Carl Friedrich Keil and Franz Delitzsch, *Biblical Commentary on The Books of Samuel*, Commentaries on the Old Testament (Grand Rapids, MI: Eerdmans, 1963), 241–42.

4. *Hamilton: An American Musical*, Kail.

Chapter 9

1. Kenneth E. Bailey, *Through Peasant Eyes: A Literary-Cultural Approach to the Parables in Luke* (Grand Rapids, MI: Eerdmans, 1983), 3.

2. Leon Morris, *Luke*, Tyndale New Testament Commentaries Vol. 3 (Downers Grove, IL: Intervarsity Press, 2008), 166.

3. Bailey, *Through Peasant Eyes*, 3.

4. Bailey, *Through Peasant Eyes*, 9.

5. Bailey, *Through Peasant Eyes*, 8.

6. Morris, *Luke*, 168.

7. John Piper, "Luke 7:36–50, Part 2: God's Love for the Worst," Desiring God, September 24, 2015, https://www.desiringgod.org/labs/gods-love-for-the-worst.

Chapter 10

1. Kenneth E. Bailey, *Through Peasant Eyes: A Literary-Cultural Approach to the Parables in Luke* (Grand Rapids, MI: Eerdmans, 1983), 12.

2. Simon Kistemaker, *The Parables of Jesus* (Grand Rapids, MI: Baker Books, 1980), 160.

3. Bailey, *Through Peasant Eyes*, 4.

4. Bailey, *Through Peasant Eyes*, 4.

5. Bailey, *Through Peasant Eyes*, 5.

6. L. Levison, *The Parables: Their Background and Local Setting* (Edinburgh: T. and T. Clark, 1926), in Bailey, *Through Peasant Eyes*, 8.

7. Bailey, *Through Peasant Eyes*, 16.

8. Bailey, *Through Peasant Eyes*, 17.

9. E. Earle Ellis, *The Gospel of Luke*, New Century Bible Commentaries (Grand Rapids, MI: Eerdmans, 1981), 122.

10. Dane Calvin Ortlund, *Gentle and Lowly: The Heart of Christ for Sinners and Sufferers* (Wheaton, IL: Crossway, 2020), 148–49.

11. Robert D. Jones, *Pursuing Peace: A Christian Guide to Handling Our Conflicts* (Wheaton, IL: Crossway, 2012), 141.

Chapter 11

1. Stephen Viars, *Overcoming Bitterness: Moving from Life's Greatest Hurts to a Life Filled with Joy* (Grand Rapids: Baker Books, a division of Baker Publishing Group, 2021), 170.

2. Brother Lawrence, *The Practice of the Presence of God* (Westwood, NJ: Fleming H. Revell Company, 1958), 6–7.

3. Lawrence, *The Practice of the Presence of God*, 39.

Chapter 12

1. Joyce Baldwin, *1 and 2 Samuel: An Introduction and Commentary*, Tyndale Old Testament Commentaries Vol. 8 (Downers Grove, IL: InterVarsity Press, 1988), 164.

2. Robert D. Bergen, *1, 2 Samuel*, The New American Commentary 7 (Nashville, TN: Broadman & Holman, 1996), 253.

3. Dane Calvin Ortlund, *Gentle and Lowly: The Heart of Christ for Sinners and Sufferers* (Wheaton, IL: Crossway, 2020), 19.

4. Bergen, *1, 2 Samuel*, 261–62.

5. Bergen, *1, 2 Samuel*, 264.

6. Howard Frederic Vos, *1, 2 Samuel: Bible Study Commentary*, Bible Study Commentary Series (Grand Rapids, MI: Zondervan, 1983), 96.

7. Baldwin, *1 and 2 Samuel*, 177.

8. Baldwin, *1 and 2 Samuel*, 178.

9. Bergen, *1, 2 Samuel*, 276.

10. Baldwin, *1 and 2 Samuel*, 181.

11. Baldwin, *1 and 2 Samuel*, 8:178.

12. Vos, *1, 2 Samuel*, 96.

Appendix 1

1. I am completely indebted to these people for the content of this appendix: Kïrsten Christianson, Joy Forrest, Darby Strickland, Jeremy Pierre, Curtis Solomon, and Greg Wilson.

2. Called to Peace Ministries, "Warning Signs Quiz," 2020, https://www.calledtopeace.org/resources/warning-signs-quiz/.

3. Darby Strickland, "How to Discern True Repentance When Serious Sin Has Occurred," *Journal of Biblical Counseling* 34, no. 3 (2020), 30–47.

Appendix 2

1. Robert W. Yarbrough, *The Letters to Timothy and Titus*, The Pillar New Testament Commentary (Grand Rapids, MI: Eerdmans, 2018), 479.

Appendix 3

1. Gerhard Kittel, Gerhard Friedrich, and Geoffrey William Bromiley, eds., *Theological Dictionary of the New Testament* (Grand Rapids: Eerdmans, 1985), 606.

2. Kittel, Friedrich, and Bromiley, 918; Frederick W. Danker, Walter Bauer, and William Arndt, *A Greek-English Lexicon of the New Testament and Other Early Christian Literature*, 3rd ed. (Chicago: University of Chicago Press, 2000), 854.

3. D. A. Carson, *Exegetical Fallacies*, 2nd ed. (Grand Rapids: Baker Books, 1996), 33–35.

4. John M. Frame, *The Doctrine of the Christian Life*, A Theology of Lordship (Phillipsburg, NJ: P & R Publishing, 2008), 774–76; Jim Newheiser, *Marriage, Divorce, and Remarriage: Critical Questions and Answers* (Phillipsburg, NJ: P & R Publishing, 2017), 240–42.